Ukraine and the Art of Strategy

Ukraine and the Art of Strategy

LAWRENCE FREEDMAN

OXFORD
UNIVERSITY PRESS

OXFORD
UNIVERSITY PRESS

Oxford University Press is a department of the University of Oxford. It furthers the University's objective of excellence in research, scholarship, and education by publishing worldwide. Oxford is a registered trade mark of Oxford University Press in the UK and certain other countries.

Published in the United States of America by Oxford University Press
198 Madison Avenue, New York, NY 10016, United States of America.

© Oxford University Press 2019

Library of Congress Cataloging-in-Publication Data
Names: Freedman, Lawrence, author.
Title: Ukraine and the art of strategy / Lawrence Freedman.
Description: New York, NY : Oxford University Press, [2019]
Identifiers: LCCN 2018020914| ISBN 9780190902889 (hardcover) |
ISBN 9780190902896 (updf) | ISBN 9780190902902 (epub)
Subjects: LCSH: Ukraine—Strategic aspects. | Ukraine Conflict, 2014- |
Russia (Federation)—Military policy. | Ukraine—Foreign relations—
Russia (Federation) | Russia (Federation)—Foreign relations—Ukraine.
Classification: LCC UA829.U4 F74 2019 | DDC 947.7086—dc23
LC record available at https://lccn.loc.gov/2018020914

9 8 7 6 5 4 3

Printed by Integrated Books International, United States of America

TABLE OF CONTENTS

ACKNOWLEDGMENTS

This work began with a graduate seminar organized by Christine Cheng and was helped on its way by feedback from Christine and Tim Sweijs. Ryan Evans provided me with the opportunity to try out my developing thoughts on the Ukrainian conflict on his excellent site, War on the Rocks, and then Dana Allin and Matthew Harries encouraged me to turn them into pieces for the journal *Survival*. This series of articles benefitted from comments by Ian Kearns and Theo Farrell, while Nicholas Marsh of the Peace Research Institute Oslo (PRIO) kept me and others well supplied with up-to-date material on the conflict in Ukraine. Anne Applebaum and Alexander Clarkson offered helpful comments on the book manuscript. It has been a pleasure to work again with my editor David McBride and his excellent team at OUP.

Ukraine and the Art of Strategy

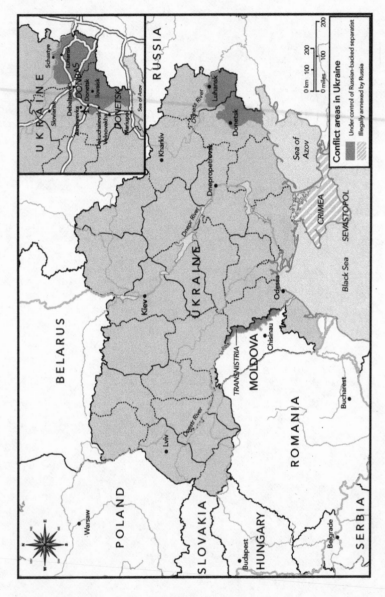

Map 1

Introduction

'You Can't Always Get What You Want'
ROLLING STONES, *Let It Bleed*, 1969

On March 18, 2014, President Vladimir Putin of Russia announced that Crimea, which had been part of Ukraine, was now part of Russia. This was territory seized by Russian Special Forces acting with local separatists at the end of February. Soon a similar combination of forces was at work in Eastern Ukraine. While these efforts did not lead to further annexations, separatist enclaves were established with Russian support in the Donbas region.

The action was taken because Russia faced an abrupt loss of influence in Ukraine following a successful uprising against President Viktor Yanukovych. The trigger was clear enough. Less clear were Putin's objectives. One view was that Moscow hoped to foster a broad-based movement opposed to those taking power in the capital, Kiev. Perhaps such a movement could put irresistible pressure on the new Ukrainian government to back away from its pro-Western course. Alternatively, the hope might have been that parts of Ukraine, particularly the old territory of Novorossiya, might then attach themselves in some way to Russia. Whatever the original aspiration, by the spring of 2014 Russian efforts were concentrated in the two Donbas enclaves of Donetsk and Luhansk (Donbas refers to the "Donetsk Coal Basin"). A Ukrainian "Anti-Terrorist Operation" looked like it might take back the lost territory, prompting a more overt Russian intervention using regular forces, which reinforced and consolidated the separatist enclaves. A cease-fire was agreed on in Minsk in September 2014, which also outlined the basis of an eventual peace settlement. The enclaves, but not Crimea, would revert to Ukraine. In return, the region would have more autonomy. This approach was confirmed in February 2015, also at Minsk, but was not implemented. Instead, there was a stalemate, with regular fighting and casualties. The boundaries of the enclaves moved but not by much.

When the conflict first broke, there were concerns that this could be the start of something much bigger. NATO countries challenged the annexation, and Russia was condemned at the UN Security Council (although its veto ensured that it was not censured in a resolution). Moscow responded with threats to other neighboring states and made references to its nuclear strength, raising the political temperature across Europe and causing NATO to look to its own preparedness for war and the need to shore up deterrence. Countries such as Estonia stressed their vulnerability to Russian aggression. Neutral states such as Sweden and Finland began to consider whether they should join NATO. Scares about a wider military conflict eventually subsided, but the measures and countermeasures continued to have deep and significant effects. Western sanctions combined with a fall in the oil price hurt Russia's economic performance. Russia's attempts to sow divisions and encourage the rise of parties in the West more sympathetic to its concerns became a major issue, especially when US intelligence agencies reported on the ways in which Russia had attempted to influence the outcome of the 2016 presidential election.

This conflict was a product of the post–Cold War order. Prior to the end of 1991, when the Soviet Union split into fifteen independent republics, any action ordered by Moscow to get Ukraine into line would have been considered the Soviet Union's own business. Western states would have commented adversely but without any basis on which to get involved. For example, as late as January 1991 the Soviet leadership used force to restrain Lithuanian demands for independence with only muffled Western criticism. Yet by the end of that year the Soviet Union was no more, and Lithuania became an independent country. In 2004 it joined NATO, gaining the protections of alliance and also became part of the EU. Ukraine, once it became a sovereign, independent state, could in principle follow the same path and join whatever alliances and economic organizations it chose. But Russia was never at ease with the idea of an independent Ukraine. Instead it sought to draw it back into a closer relationship. The 2014 crisis erupted when this effort failed. What would once have been an internal matter for the Soviet Union was now a matter of international concern.

Just before this crisis came to a head, I published a book on the history of the concept of strategy and how it had come to be applied in a number of settings.[1] I suggested that strategies should be evaluated by comparing the actual outcome of conflicts with the outcomes that might have been anticipated by looking at the balance of power at their start (hence it was about "creating power"). As the Ukraine crisis broke and became more severe, this case appeared relevant to my approach to strategy as practice. Not only were the affected countries entering uncharted territory, requiring a substantial degree of improvisation, but also the comparative strategic performance by the key actors was being evaluated. There was more at stake with the Russo-Ukraine conflict than just the future of those two countries. NATO was not directly engaged in the fighting, but it had to consider whether and how it might seek to influence events and prepare for future escalation.

President Putin was commended as a more accomplished strategist than the US president Barack Obama. The political scientist John Mearsheimer described Putin as "a first-class strategist who should be feared and respected by anyone challenging him on foreign policy."[2] Putin was already said to have bested Obama over Syria in September 2013, when the US president held back after the Syrian government crossed a prior "red line" by using chemical weapons, and Russia then moved in to provide him with a diplomatic way out. This made the United States look weak and Russia strong. That November, Putin had also apparently pulled Ukraine away from the EU into Russia's sphere of influence. While this was repudiated by a strong, determined, and ultimately successful movement in Ukraine, the resolute nature of the Russian response after President Yanukovych fled the country drew a sort of grudging admiration, even from Putin's detractors. He showed that he was prepared to use military as well as diplomatic and economic means to pursue his agenda. Western countries were left flat-footed, desperately trying to come up with a response that did not make a bad situation worse. As time went on, however, without Russia achieving its broader goals with respect to Ukraine, Putin's strategic aptitude began to be questioned.

I was curious as to whether the body of strategic theory I had recently been studying, especially those elements developed during the Cold War, could help illuminate the conflict and suggest how it might work out. Could concepts developed for a bipolar world, dominated by two nuclear-armed superpowers and their associated alliances, help us make sense of this new state of affairs? To answer this question I presented a paper to a graduate seminar at King's College London on "Ukraine and the Art of Crisis Management." I then developed my first thoughts into a lengthy blog for the American site *War on the Rocks*. Eventually it was turned into a full-length article for the journal *Survival*, published by the International Institute for Strategic Studies. That October, after a period of intense fighting in Eastern Ukraine, I followed this up, using a similar format, with a piece on "Ukraine and the Art of Limited War." A year later, with the fighting continuing but little movement on the front lines and a diplomatic impasse, a final article examined "Ukraine and the Art of Exhaustion."[3]

These three pieces are the foundation of this book, although they have not survived the rewriting in anything like their earlier form. My original intention was to republish them as they first appeared. There might be a certain interest in seeing how events were evaluated as they occurred and not just with the benefit of hindsight. The material, however, needed to be updated, largely to reflect developments from 2015 to the start of 2018. It also needed to be made more coherent, so that there was less overlap and repetition. Originally I also intended to follow the same format, with each chapter exploring an aspect of the conflict in the light of a particular strategic concept. I decided instead to open with an essay describing the key strategic concepts emerging out of the Cold War and their potential relevance for Ukraine, before considering the strategic decision making as the conflict developed, and then returning to see what this case study might suggest about the practice of strategy.

A secondary purpose of this book is to provide a brief history of the Ukraine conflict in the context of the various tensions that have developed in and around the former Soviet Union since the end of the Cold War. I do not claim expertise in either Russia or Ukraine, and so, as always when I write about countries and regions that interest me, I draw on the scholarship and expertise of others. This book therefore does not claim to provide a full history of relations between Russia and Ukraine, or even of this particular period. There are now many books that do this very well.[4] A number of these address the question of who is the most to blame, making points about either Western double standards in supporting Ukraine or pusillanimity in not doing so sufficiently.[5] My main purpose, however, is to explore problems of strategy: How did the various actors identify their objectives and seek to achieve them, and to what extent were they successful?

This conflict has been seen as a test bed for modern warfare. In particular, the Russian approach has been described as innovative in its ability to merge the overt and the covert, combining regular with irregular forces in the field, and in its use of its own propaganda outlets along with more seditious social media campaigns to undermine the confidence of opponents while sustaining morale at home. For their part, Western countries have relied extensively on sanctions and have tried to refine them to be not such blunt instruments that punish whole societies for the actions of their elites. Instead, they target the elites themselves. Whether those innovations made much difference is one of the issues for this book. Despite the various efforts put into developing a range of coercive measures, the basic parameters of the conflict were set in the six months from Yanukovych's flight to the first Minsk agreement. Although great efforts were then made at high human costs to change these parameters, they then barely moved. The belligerents found it hard to move forward even though at the same time they were able to resist being pushed back. Over this period, the wider consequences in terms of Russia's international relations, or the influence of its information campaigns on American politics, were more profound. The conflict over Ukraine was not by itself responsible for Russia's emergence as a champion of hardline nationalist movements in Europe and North America, nor the election victory of Donald Trump, a man sympathetic to these movements and skeptical of his country's traditional alliances. But it is an important part of this much wider story.

This case therefore tells us something about modern warfare, the exercise of coercive power, and the role of influence campaigns. The conclusions are far less dramatic than the hyperbole surrounding these innovations suggests. In those areas where "hard" military and economic power makes a difference, it can overwhelm "softer" forms of power. Unsurprisingly, in straight fights the stronger tend to prevail over the weaker. In contests over territory, raw military strength determines how much can be taken and held, but that will be of limited value in determining how well the territory in question is governed. Forms of coercion tend to be better at deterring than compelling; economic coercion can make a real difference against a weak target but less so against a strong one. But if the coercer overreaches, the target might be destabilized. Information campaigns tend to reinforce existing trends in popular opinion rather than create them, although that may be sufficient to turn a difficult situation into a transformational moment. In some respects the Ukraine case does point to a different future, but it has also been marked by continuity with past conflicts.

Strategic Theory

During the period from the Napoleonic Wars to the First World War, the conceptual framework surrounding the conduct of war was bound up with the idea of a decisive battle. Once its army had been defeated in battle, the enemy would have little choice but to accept the political terms imposed by the victors. Thus simplified military strategy was focused on getting forces into a position to fight their battles. How they fought was a matter for tactics. Why they fought was a matter for policy. Military thought tended to focus on the interaction between tactics and strategy, and what officers needed to understand in order to be proficient in both. By the start of the twentieth century, more interest was being shown in the question of the interaction between policy and strategy as it became apparent that peacetime preparations might make all the difference to who would prevail in war.

The First World War led to three big changes in the way that strategy was understood. First, battle was recognized to be a means to an end and not an end in itself. Second, military strategy could not therefore be considered separate from the requirements of policy. Third, following from this, there was a need for "grand strategy," which was the level at which all instruments of policy, including the economic and the diplomatic as well as the military, had to be brought together in order to prepare for war and then prosecute a war effectively.

This released thinking about strategy from its overdependence on battle and encouraged consideration of the wider context when thinking about issues of war and peace. It also led to a hierarchical approach. It fitted best a model that had decisions cascading down from governments responsible for grand strategy, commanders in chief turning policy objectives into strategy, theater commanders turning strategy into operations, and then local commanders turning operations into tactics. As evidence from encounters with the enemy moved back up the chain of command, adjustments should take place, on occasion leading to reappraisals of objectives and the means available to achieve them. With variations in types of military operations, many limited in scope and objectives, and with individual encounters depending on local knowledge and initiative, this hierarchy began to creak. It became dysfunctional if followed too rigidly.

Over time, strategy lost focus. Leaving aside the obvious point that the word was used regularly in nonmilitary settings, such as business and domestic politics, even when employed in a military setting it covered an expanding range of contingencies, from nuclear war to counterinsurgency campaigns to stabilizing war-torn societies. A grand strategy that ensured credible preparations for a future war could mean that war was avoided altogether by deterring a potential adversary. Once a conflict had begun to acquire economic and diplomatic dimensions, these might not reinforce military action but influence events separately—and so require strategies of their own. Grand strategy became detached from preparations for the conduct of war and merged into the general foreign policy to achieve political goals without recourse to war.

The Cold War between the US and the Soviet Union that began after World War II involved a strategic problem that remained relatively unchanged over four decades—a deep ideological antagonism that, if taken too far, could lead to a nuclear conflagration, obliterating both superpowers and their allies, and much else besides. An uneasy stalemate developed. This fear of both war and of appeasement encouraged a search for ways to deal with political differences, even those that appeared quite fundamental, by employing means other than direct violence, such as diplomatic isolation and economic sanctions, and to forms of restraint and limitation in the conduct of war.

This tension prompted a period of remarkable innovation in strategic theory. Many of the concepts developed during the 1950s and 1960s continue to influence our thinking not only about war and peace but also about everyday strategic discourse. This can be seen in regular references to "escalation," "crisis management," "damage limitation," "zero-sum games," and "worst-case scenarios." Even concepts with a longer lineage such as "deterrence" and "limited war" gained new meaning and prominence during the Cold War.

While nuclear weapons are still a vital and terrifying feature of contemporary international affairs, the Cold War is long past. Relations between states, and also within them, have become more fluid and complex. There are new challenges to be faced, as different cultures and political systems grind against each other, and new methods of disrupting and coercing have emerged. Russia's attempts to shape events in Ukraine have involved the whole range of contemporary instruments of conflict, from nuclear threats to direct intervention to covert operations to economic pressure to information operations. These are often mentioned now as representing a step change in strategic practice, suggesting that the old concepts no longer work and have been superseded. Before considering the extent to which this is so, I will examine some of the intellectual legacy of the Cold War in strategic thought.

CRISIS MANAGEMENT

Strategy is a noun and not a verb, something one has rather than does. A strategy tends to be presented as a plan to be followed, a description of actions leading to a specified goal. Strategies fail because once a conflict begins, other actors, supposed allies as well as adversaries, have opportunities to interfere in a plan's implementation. There is therefore a dynamic aspect to strategy requiring an active engagement with changing circumstances. Regular adjustments become necessary in response to events and better knowledge about the strategies of other significant actors. There is therefore a difference between having a strategy, which suggests a plan, and acting strategically, which suggests flexibility and responding to events. Of course, it may be best to act strategically after a period of deliberation during which alternative courses of action are evaluated, but that is not always possible because others may have taken the initiative, or be about to do so. A strategy may have to be improvised under the pressure of urgent events. Intuition may play as important a role as deliberation.

When established positions are suddenly challenged and it becomes necessary to respond quickly to unexpected events, there is a crisis. The Greek word *krisis* referred to a turning point in a disease, as when the fever reached a peak and the patient was either going to get a lot worse or a lot better. Crises eventually came to refer to moments of great difficulty or danger, stress, and urgency. It meant that a conflict had come to a head, normally because one side had taken a bold but provocative initiative. At the moment of crisis, some big, long-standing conflict was about to be resolved—either through last-minute diplomacy or by force. The drama came from a deadline, perhaps reinforced by an ultimatum, and intense media attention, with late nights in the corridors of power, emergency summits, tense Security Council meetings, and reports of military mobilizations and movements. Crises would test the mettle of the leaders of major powers, demanding a steely resolve and calm judgment. The right temperament was essential. This was the point of Hillary Clinton's famous challenge to candidate Barack Obama in 2008 as to how he would cope when "It's 3 a.m. and your children are safe and asleep. But there's a phone in the White House and its ringing. Something's happening in the world."[1]

Half a century ago, after the conflicts over Berlin and Cuba, a new term of art came into vogue—"crisis management." In a number of respects, the term and the key themes it invoked were behind much of the debate on security policy for the remainder of the Cold War.[2] The US secretary of defense Robert McNamara was even quoted as saying that crisis management had taken over from strategy. If McNamara did say this, it was misleading.[3] Good crisis management required good strategy. The special challenge lay in producing it in stressful conditions, under severe time constraints, without the opportunities for careful deliberation and consultation, in circumstances in which poor moves and inappropriate language might be inflammatory and counterproductive. Should the original crisis turn into something longer lasting, as happened with Ukraine, new strategies would soon be needed. These could be constructed with greater care and attention, but still within the limits set by first moves.

The most toxic term used to describe crisis management was "brinkmanship." Its origins can be traced to Secretary of State John Foster Dulles, who remarked in 1956 that "The ability to get to the verge without getting into the war is the necessary art. If you cannot master it, you inevitably get into war. If you try to run away from it, if you are scared to go to the brink, you are lost."[4] Thereafter "brinkmanship" was used to refer to a reckless foreign policy.[5] Governments would not actually wish to go over the brink, but creating the impression that they might nonetheless do so risked either incredibility or unintended disaster. This led to characterizations of subsequent Cold War crises in the terms of a game of chicken, normally presented as two juveniles pointing cars at each other to see who would swerve first. As the Cuban Missile Crisis played out in October 1962, the game of chicken, or some variant, came to mind, captured in Secretary of State Dean Rusk's remark as Soviet ships decided not to run the US blockade, that "we've been eyeball to eyeball and I think the other fellow just blinked." The mythology of the Cuban Missile Crisis overstated the importance of firm "red lines" and steely resolve while understating the need to beware the misapprehensions and miscalculations of crises and the need to think about diplomatic exit routes.[6]

It is unavoidable that at times of crisis the personalities of key actors will be scrutinized, especially if there are signs of panic or unwarranted bravado. But crises are much more than tests of character. Good strategy depends on understanding the crisis's meaning for all participants and identifying appropriate options that can look after core interests without pushing others into drastic and harmful action. One lesson drawn from Cuba, for example, was the need to help an adversary back away from the brink without being humiliated in the process. In retrospect fifty years after the crisis, a key factor enabling its resolution was described as "the willingness of each side to allow the other a face-saving way out of the crisis."[7] Yet in subsequent crises it was not always obvious how this could be achieved. It meant identifying a feature of the crisis that was vital to the opponent but not to you. With a trivial gesture no face would be saved.

Successful crisis management therefore requires clarity about core interests. Thus in the case of the Berlin Crisis, the other dangerous confrontation of the early 1960s, the US was, in principle, committed to keeping Berlin as an open city. In practice, however, President Kennedy accepted that the core interest was West Berlin, and that limited the risks he was prepared to take on behalf of those already living under Communism in the East. So while the erection of the Berlin Wall of August 1961 was a blow to the cause of German reunification, and to East Germans, it also defused the crisis.[8]

How one crisis is managed is regularly assumed to affect the ability to manage the next, as reputations for resolve and strategic acuity are shaped. Might Putin, for example, have been more careful when moving against Ukraine had the 2013 events in Syria not led him to conclude that President Obama was cautious and risk averse? The danger with such arguments is that they can lead to taking more risks than may be wise to avoid perceptions of weakness. This comes back to clarity on interests. By and large, dealing with the matter at hand on its own terms will make the most sense rather than using every opportunity to demonstrate toughness. In some settings this might be possible, because of a superior position. But in others, where good options are scarce, then prudence will dictate caution. That being said, crises do have to be managed with an eye to the future. They provide case law for later crises. Their most prominent aspects, however unique, will invariably be analyzed for "lessons." They provide the precedents to which governments return when seeking to rationalize their decisions or to demonstrate that opponents are hypocrites.

The impact of crisis management on the perceptions of allies will always be an issue for the United States. No other country is so important to the security of so many others, and for that reason its performance is continually monitored by allies. The somewhat contradictory performance criteria by which the US is evaluated involve a readiness to honor commitments while not making situations more dangerous than they already are when doing so. This requires being ready to resort to armed force but not rushing to do so. Threats of force can serve diplomacy but should not force its pace. This was the lesson of 1914, when the demanding mobilization timetable for the German offensive became a serious destabilizing factor. The fearful prospect of a nuclear equivalent, as the US and the Soviet Union wondered about each other's ability to mount a preemptive first strike, led to the idea of "crisis stability" as a key objective of arms control. For true crisis stability there must be no lasting advantages in launching a surprise attack, so there is no need to dash to war. There should be time to deliberate and negotiate. Related to this was the need for disciplined armed forces so that not even the smallest unit would get involved in an incident that could trigger something wider and more dangerous. Avoiding escalation through inadvertence required continuing communications and diplomatic activity during a crisis, whether through intermediaries, meetings at the foreign minister level, or direct conversations between leaders.

After the missile crisis one former American diplomat, Harlan Cleveland, advised that its lessons were to control a crisis's development by keeping objectives limited, deciding in advance how far to go, creeping up carefully on the use of force, and drawing others into the issue ("widen the community of the concerned"). On the character issue he observed: "It takes no courage to bluster; it takes some to stand up to a mortal threat that plainly has to be faced. But what takes the most gumption is to persevere in a decision that takes months or years to prove itself."[9] The last point is important. The idea of a crisis is of a moment when things get a whole lot better or a whole lot worse, when matters get resolved one way or the other. It may, however, just represent a moment of discontinuity. Past assumptions and arrangements may be challenged and replaced, but these underlying issues left unresolved provide a continuing basis for conflict. Crises often lose their edge and drama, moving from front-page headlines to occasional updates on the news pages. At some point it becomes apparent that a particular conflict, even if it has taken a turn for the worse, is going to remain within manageable boundaries. However miserable life may be for those directly involved, the risk of others being drawn in subsides. It becomes normalized, and so a part of the international environment that governments must recognize and work around. This creates its own challenges for foreign policy because while the conflict remains active, so too do the stances taken when it first appeared in the form of a crisis.

DETERRENCE

The purpose of deterrence is to avoid crises by warning of the dire consequences of disruptive behavior. Deterrence became the preferred Western strategy during the Cold War. The Soviet Union was warned of the severe risks—including nuclear war—it would run with any aggressive action. The attraction of deterrence was that governments could present it as being defensive but not weak, and firm but not reckless. It offered the prospect of controlling security threats without actually fighting. It was in some ways the perfect strategy, for while it worked nothing happened and no further measures needed to be taken. But until deterrent threats were tested there would always be doubts about their credibility. Strategic discourse focused on how to ensure that they were taken seriously.[10] If the adversary decided that deterrence was a bluff, then a crisis might erupt and the issue would soon become one of whether the threats were to be implemented, and whether it would do much good if they were.

Because Cold War deterrence was generally held to have worked well, the approach acquired a positive aura. The new set of security challenges that emerged after 1990 raised the question of whether comparable results could be achieved through reconceptualizing deterrence. The two sets of circumstances, however, appeared very different. Cold War deterrence was about superpower confrontations and nuclear exchanges. Now the threats were many and varied, posed by states, large and small, nonstate actors, and even individuals, such as "lone-wolf" terrorists. When national survival and the integrity of alliances were at stake, it could be assumed that any direct challenges would be taken seriously even when responses were fraught with danger. Could the same be assumed when the challenges were to lesser interests?

Reconceptualizing deterrence required detaching it from its association with nuclear threats. Once that was done, the concept could be relevant to a range of cases and work in a variety of ways. Here is a simple definition of deterrence from Alexander George and Richard Smoke:

> Deterrence is simply the persuasion of one's opponent that
> the costs and/or risks of a given course of action he might
> take outweigh its benefits.[11]

This cost/benefit definition might cover the manipulation of likely benefits as well as likely costs. Encouraging the opponent to reappraise any aggressive plans by threatening to block offensive action (denial) is as plausible and in many ways more satisfactory than threatening severe pain (punishment).[12] In addition, the quality of denial can be measured in more physical terms. Calculating the amount of military effort required to hold on to a piece of territory may not be an exact science, but it is still more straightforward than an attempt to discern the effect of prospective punitive measures on an opponent's decision making.[13] It also offers a greater hope of retrieving the situation if the opponent presses on regardless.

For deterrence to work, the target must recognize the risks of ignoring or discounting threats. Crafting deterrence strategies therefore requires an insight into the target's risk calculus. This may not always be too difficult. When faced with the possibility of nuclear war, states that vary hugely in circumstances, cultures, and ideologies may all still tend to act like a cautious "rational actor." Their distinctive characteristics are likely to be much more important when the contingencies are more nuanced and the interests engaged less stark.

It should be obvious when a deterrence strategy has failed: a line will be crossed. So long as the line is not crossed it will be assumed that the strategy is succeeding. There can, however, be a number of explanations for the target's inaction. It might never have intended to cross the line, or had thought about it and decided not to do so for reasons quite separate from any deterrent threats, or if it had been deterred this was because it perceived threats separate from the ones upon which the deterrer was depending. There is therefore a distinction between deterrence as strategic intent and deterrence as strategic effect. Deterrent threats can be issued that have no effect, while deterrent effects can occur without threats being issued. Deterrence happens all the time without much prompting, but when there is a prompt it may nonetheless fail.

The purpose of a deterrent strategy is to stabilize situations. If they stay stable then the strategy will be declared successful, though over time stability may be the result less of specific threats and more inertia and loss of interest. As a situation becomes unstable and dangerous, and moves toward crisis, deterrence becomes more important but also more difficult. Indeed, when deterrence is at its most urgent it is most likely to fail. In the face of new and specific challenges, interests must be defined with clarity and then asserted with conviction, warnings conveyed with credibility, and relevant capabilities conspicuously prepared. While this is going on, the challenge may be changing in direction and intensity, fortified by uncertainties surrounding these warnings and commitments.

A sudden challenge may raise questions about whether a particular interest really is vital, but simply because it is being challenged it cannot be ignored or played down. Because all interests are not of equal worth, it is unwise to make them all subjects of deterrence. At the high end of major war the workings of deterrence are easy to grasp. The prospect of major war, with all the chaos, death, and destruction that would entail, is a deterrent in itself. This is why NATO still has an important function as its Article 5 provision commits each member state to consider an armed attack against one member state, in Europe or North America, to be an armed attack against them all. This creates a risk that what might otherwise have been a localized incident can be turned into a general war. It is notable that Russia was prepared to invade Ukraine and Georgia, which are not part of NATO, rather than Estonia and Latvia, which are.

COERCIVE DIPLOMACY

Not all security challenges can be anticipated and then deterred in advance. When deterrence fails, or when faced with a conflict that has suddenly taken an unexpected and dangerous turn, policy makers may look to coercive diplomacy to retrieve the situation.[14] Instead of making threats to persuade the target not to act, the challenge is now to get the target to act and abandon whatever gains had been made. The Oxford English Dictionary defines coercion as "the application of force to control the action of a voluntary agent." The key to coercion is that the target is a voluntary agent—and so retains choice. Coercion therefore requires influencing another's decision making. It depends on how the target's decision making is understood (Is there really a supreme leader? Who are the most influential voices in the inner circles of government?), and whether persuasive forms of pressure can be devised. These must not only be impressive on their own but also be able to compete with other pressures faced by these decision makers and shape the way they construct reality. Of all the many and sometimes contradictory pressures in play this must be the one that demands the target's attention. To get the target to the point where it must choose compliance with the coercer's demands, there might have to be a process of testing, so that it comes to appreciate the pressure and recognize to where it is leading. This may involve negotiation, informal as well as formal, perhaps conducted at a distance, through public statements and gestures as much as private discussions or through third-party mediation. The demands must take a form that can be met and which are proportionate to the threats.

In this respect the key feature of coercion is that it is unlikely to achieve what the OED definition suggests is its object—that of control. So long as an agent's actions are voluntary they are not truly controlled. A voluntary agent has choices, and this means options to ignore, deflect, or modify the demands of the coercer as well as to acquiesce in them. Coercion occupies part of a spectrum marked by consent at one end and control at the other, reflecting an actor's expectations of the responsiveness of another to its requirements, and thus the necessity to use force to impose its will. When force and other forms of active pressure are not required, then there can be a presumption of consent; when no compliance is anticipated and overwhelming force is applied, control has been taken and choice has been denied. Coercion lacks the legitimacy provided by consent or the certainty promised by control. Unsuccessful coercion may therefore necessitate a more aggressive approach based on control or else a more conciliatory approach geared to generating consent.

This distinction between control and coercion is illuminated by Tom Schelling. It is

between taking what you want and making someone give it to you, between fending off assault and making someone afraid to assault you, between holding what people are trying to take and making them afraid to take it, between losing what someone can forcibly take and giving it up to avoid risk or damage. It is the difference between defense and deterrence, between brute force and intimidation, between conquest and blackmail, between actions and threats. It is the difference between the unilateral, "undiplomatic" recourse to strength, and coercive diplomacy based on the power to hurt.[15]

Deterrence is a form of coercion but, as Schelling also explained, this is essentially defensive. He distinguished it from compellence, which is essentially offensive. Thus a forcible offense is taking something, occupying a place or disarming an enemy by some direct action that the enemy is unable to block. By contrast compellence is

inducing his withdrawal or his acquiescence, or his
collaboration by an action that threatens to hurt, often
one that could not forcibly accomplish its aim but that,
nevertheless, can hurt enough to induce compliance.[16]

Deterrence involves a demand of inaction; compellence a demand of action. Deterrence involves explaining what must not
be done and the consequences if it is—and then waiting. The
overt act is up to the opponent. Acts of compellence, in contrast,
only cease when the opponent complies satisfactorily with the
demands. In a conflict in which both sides can hurt each other
but neither can forcibly accomplish its purpose, then what is
compellent and deterrent can shift for both sides over time. After
Russia's initial moves against Ukraine, deterrence was applied in
terms of efforts to establish limits on the conflict. NATO warned
Russia about further aggression, especially into NATO countries;
Russian warned Ukraine about attempting to take back what it
had lost. By this time, however, some of the conflict's most important features involved compellence, in terms of the pressure
put on Ukraine to accede to Russian demands and then the pressure put on Russia to back off. Deterrence would have said, "Do
not annex Crimea or else"; compellence said, "You must release
Crimea from annexation or else."

Deterrence works best when set in place long before a crisis
erupts, while compellence tends to come into play during a crisis,
although in circumstances where it may only succeed with overwhelming power. Compellence involves demanding that a move
already made must be reversed and so adding to the loss of a gain
an additional loss of face. This contrasts with deterrence when
the opponent may stay inactive and deny that any aggressive act

was ever contemplated. With compellence, Schelling observed, compliance "is likely to be less casual, less capable of being rationalized as something that one was going to do anyhow".[17] Thus the act of definite compliance may be in itself a form of humiliation and an acknowledgment of submission. This is why its long-term consequences might be found not only in the power relationship between the adversaries but also in their respective reputations for resolve. They do not want to be seen as "soft touches" or unable to drive hard bargains.

Although the term "compellence" has value, these days it tends to be used only by those exploring Schelling's framework. A more common term to describe more or less the same phenomenon is "coercive diplomacy," devised by Alexander George, another giant of postwar strategic studies. Whereas Schelling was trying to think through the impact of nuclear weapons on strategic theory, George was heavily influenced by the failed American effort to coerce North Vietnam during the 1960s. According to George:

> The general intent of coercive diplomacy is to back a demand on an adversary with a threat of punishment for noncompliance that will be credible and potent enough to persuade him that it is in his interest to comply with the demand.

The challenge for those employing coercive diplomacy was one of finding a way to "inject" the message of the threats "into the adversary's calculations and lead him to comply with the demand made." Relevant factors would include the nature of the demand, an assessment of the adversary's determination and

also of whether "the threatened punishment is sufficiently credible and potent to cause him to comply." This argued for the
coercer to frame demands carefully, create an appropriate sense
of urgency, pick the right form of punishment, add positive
inducements, and be prepared to alter these ingredients as a crisis
unfolded.[18] As with deterrence, a key factor in determining success would be a clear objective and a strong motivation to achieve
it. George concluded that coercive diplomacy could constitute "a
high-confidence strategy in few crises," but was often difficult
to "employ successfully against a recalcitrant or unpredictable
opponent."[19]

George described three variants of coercive diplomacy: (1)
"try and see," making a demand, perhaps combined with a limited threat or action, and then waiting to see what happens;
(2) "gradual turning of the screw," using a metaphor from me-
dieval torture. The threat here, conveyed at the outset and then
carried out incrementally, was to step up the pressure by stages;
(3) "ultimatum," the starkest variant because it involved setting a
deadline for compliance. All approaches need only involve "just
enough force of an appropriate kind to demonstrate resolution
and to give credibility to the threat that greater force will be used
if necessary."[20]

One of the problems with any use of force, however, is that the
most moderate goal may have to be backed with extremely tough
action. A potent threat that any adversary should take seriously
can be undermined by evident tentativeness and hesitation. The
amount of force necessary will, to an important extent, depend
on the capacity of the target to resist. In this respect coercion is
no different from any other use of the military instrument, in
that effectiveness requires paying attention to operational and

logistical factors. There will be implementation costs that the coercer has to keep in mind, just as the target will have to recognize that the costs of resistance will need to be added to those incurred complying with the coercer's demands. Even threats cannot be a constant: logistical factors may mean that military options cannot be maintained indefinitely. Some are highly perishable: as they deteriorate so do those bargaining positions they were designed to support. Forces at high states of readiness, perhaps some distance from home base, can be hard to sustain over time.

Punitive measures raise moral issues. These are self-evident when one moves to air raids and nuclear strikes. Even with lesser measures, however, the implication is often that the pain will be imposed on the target's population. With economic sanctions, for example, the target will also have to pay resistance costs to beat them, by setting up routes for smuggling or paying above market price for essential goods. These costs reflect the central calculation that is at the heart of coercion: the effort involved in trying to prevent the imposition of pain and then the pain itself, imposed by the coercer to punish noncompliance, as against the benefits forgone or the losses accepted as a result of compliance.

The natural strategy for the target will be to seek to raise enforcement costs. This is countercoercion. The almost instinctive response of any state or group being subjected to coercive pressure is to warn of decisive rebuffs or painful reprisals, while insisting that anything that the coercer wants is nonnegotiable. In most conflicts, mutual coercion, even if somewhat one-sided, is much more likely than a wholly asymmetric relationship. Indeed a wholly asymmetric relationship would imply scant freedom of maneuver on the part of the coerced and thus control.

The quality of coercive threats and the manner of their implementation will affect the outcome of the bargaining, but there will also be other factors at play. The effectiveness of coercive strategies will depend on the overall political context in which they are implemented. A potentially promising use of force can be squandered by an ineffectual diplomacy. If the coercer's demands are neither clear nor realistic, then even a target prepared to make concessions will not know what has to be done. There are always risks of ambiguities in the message and misapprehensions. Direct communications may be advisable to ensure that both sides understand what is at stake and how events may unfold.

This brings us back to the question of choice. By conceding choice to the target, the coercer is communicating an important political message. This includes accepting that the target cannot be defeated, or only with extreme difficulty, and so its residual power must be respected and accommodated in an agreement. If the coercer demands too much, and implies that the target's regime is inherently unacceptable, then coercion is also likely to fail because any concessions are unlikely to bring relief. The key point about effective coercion is that it is about changing the policies of another state but not the regime. Its distinguishing feature is that the target is never denied choice, even if it is between the costs of compliance and of noncompliance.

ECONOMIC SANCTIONS

Economic measures are among the first to be adopted in any crisis. The aim may not necessarily be coercive. Wars make extraordinary economic demands on any country. If one is beginning or may be about to begin, all sides will have to pay attention to financing the fighting, with whom to trade, and how to obtain essential supplies. As they worry about how an enemy might try to disrupt their economies, through blockades or other military action, they will consider what harm they can do the enemy's economy. The longer a war goes on, the ability to sustain the society and the armed forces will be progressively more important.

Using economic measures on their own, not as a supplement to military measures but as an alternative, is quite common. This may be quite natural when a country is in dispute with a weaker neighbor. Trade might be disrupted quickly and without great fanfare, to make a point about dependence. This can be an effective form of coercion. As we shall see, it is an approach regularly adopted by Russia toward its neighbors. This can involve a system of rewards as well, working naturally with a system of punishments, carrots as well as sticks, in order to make sure that the target behaves appropriately. A more demanding sort of economic coercion is when one state, or group of states, imposes sanctions on another in order to persuade it to abandon some policy that is deemed threatening to international order or some cherished norms. Since the end of the Cold War, the use of economic sanctions in this way has become regular. According to one study, there were almost as many examples of economic sanctions activity in the quarter century after the end of the Cold War as there had been in the previous ninety years of the twentieth century.[21] One reason for this is that the collapse of the Soviet Union resulted in a Western hegemony over the international financial and trading systems. It became much easier to control access to these systems and impose costs on others with few negative consequences. It was preferable to use a form of pressure that did not involve direct violence.[22]

Yet while it was the case that sanctions might appear nonviolent, their practical effects could be harsh. If economic activity was effectively shut down there could be shortages of food and medical supplies, while the target regimes took care to control both smuggling and rationing to strengthen their position at the expense of their people. Hardships could be blamed on those imposing the sanctions rather than the regimes that failed to comply with their demands. They could end up encouraging corruption in the targets but also in neighboring states that became implicated in sanctions-breaking. In this respect the experience of Iraq, which was under sanctions from 1990 to 2003, had a big influence on all subsequent debates. They were first imposed in response to Iraq's invasion of Kuwait in August 1990 but stayed in place even after Kuwait had been liberated to ensure compliance with the cease-fire agreement of April 1991, which required, among other things, elimination of Iraq's weapons of mass destruction. The durability of the Iraqi regime meant that the sanctions stayed in place far longer than had been expected and were blamed for making life more miserable for the people and for high levels of infant mortality.

Even before sanctions were eventually lifted, after Iraq had been invaded in 2003, their growing unpopularity had led to consideration of a new approach. The talk was of "smart" sanctions that would be much more directed toward the perpetrators of the offending policies and the policies themselves, rather than the "dumb" version that hurt all society in an indiscriminate way.[23] They required a sophisticated understanding of financial flows and trade patterns, and also good intelligence so that the appropriate targets were properly identified. This approach was embraced by the Obama administration and applied during the Ukraine crisis. The 2015 US National Security Strategy explained the concept:

> Targeted economic sanctions remain an effective tool for imposing costs on those irresponsible actors whose military aggression, illicit proliferation, or unprovoked violence threaten both international rules and norms and the peace they were designed to preserve. We will pursue multilateral sanctions, including through the U.N., whenever possible, but will act alone, if necessary. Our sanctions will continue to be carefully designed and tailored to achieve clear aims while minimizing any unintended consequences for other economic actors, the global economy, and civilian populations.[24]

The difficulty was that there was little evidence that smart sanctions were any more effective than their dumber cousins when it came to effective coercion. The political scientist Dan Drezner sums up the conclusions of research on the general effectiveness of sanctions:

> Economic coercion appears to work better at the threat stage than at the implementation stage. On the whole, sanctions appear likely to produce concessions when the target's costs of sanctions imposition are significant, when the sender and target are closely allied, when an international institution endorses the sanctions, and when the target state is a democracy.[25]

As is the case with other forms of coercion, it is easier to deter than to compel, to persuade an opponent not to take the next step rather than to go back on a step already taken.

The challenge with smart sanctions lies with the assumptions that hurting particular individuals or activities will be sufficient to influence policy and that this can be achieved without causing more widespread pain. Drezner has described "smart or targeted sanctions" as "the precision guided munitions of economic statecraft."[26] There is a similar issue with smart sanctions as there is with precision warfare. Precision warfare provides a means of reducing the hurt to civilian populations and so moving back to more of an ideal type of decisive battle fought between regular forces. But battles are now rarely fought that way. Military precision is now often used for coercive effects, to strike specific targets linked to the leadership and their ability to run a country and fight a war. This does not mean that damage to the wider society can be avoided. At some point, for example if transport and energy supplies are targeted, this imposes pain on civil society, and if the targeting goes awry, perhaps because of faulty intelligence, then civilians are hurt directly. Alternatively precision can be used to maximize hurt and, while this is ethically and legally wrong, a case might be made that it can get a war over quickly and decisively. Similar dilemmas emerge with "smart" sanctions. Richard Nephew, a former official who worked on sanctions directed against Iran, explains:

> After all if you intentionally reduce a country's ability to earn foreign currency through exports, then you will almost by definition create at least some pressure on imports, including of food and medicine. True, a sanctioner can

always point out that it is the responsibility of the sanctioned country to manage its imports and even avoid the entire confrontation. But this does not mean that sanctions were not painful, including at the street level. Or that the sanctioner is innocent of having created any resulting crisis. Moreover, the irony of all this is that sanctions are ultimately intended to cause pain and change policy: denying some of that pain may make for better public relations for a sanctions program, but it also undermines the contention that sanctions work and may even interfere with their effectiveness on a practical level if a sanctioner adjusts the regime to address a humanitarian problem and, in doing so, reduces the very pain the sanctions are intended to create.[27]

This goes to the heart of the problem with attempting to use any coercive measures, economic or military, to influence an opponent. Unless the hurt is widespread it can be difficult to have an impact, but spreading the hurt does not look so "smart" and can appear cruel and heartless. When imposing sanctions, however tailored they may be to a particular situation, the consequences may be different from those intended.

An important qualification to this judgment is that one purpose of economic measures may not be to change the target's policy directly, or even to warn of worse to come if the target persists, but to demonstrate solidarity with the victims of this policy and recognize that some important norm has been violated. Even if they achieve little, they avoid the appearance of indifference. They provide an opportunity for a major power to show leadership and engage with partners, and in so doing increase the isolation of the target.[28]

LIMITED WARS

Coercive diplomacy assumes correspondence between how much violence is threatened or even applied and the interests at stake. The same assumption informs limited wars, that is those conducted with self-imposed restraints. Such wars are clearly not going to be "to the death," and this must restrict what can be accomplished. Wars without evident limits on what must be endured or sacrificed, because of what is at stake, are described as "existential" in that the existence of a state or a people or a way of life is at stake, which is why they may become "total" wars where all available means to defeat the enemy are employed. In more recent years a category of discretionary wars has been identified, in which there is no obligation to get involved and from which it is possible to disengage without major consequences. These are known as "wars of choice," a term that appears to have first been used by the Israeli Prime Minister Menachem Begin in August 1982 when justifying the invasion of Lebanon. The contrast was with what he called wars of "no alternative" for Israel when the ultimate security of the state was at risk.[29]

The distinction moved into general use as Western governments began to intervene in conflicts where they had no vital interests involved, for example in the former Yugoslavia. Richard Haass, a senior figure in the US government when decisions were taken to attack in Iraq in both 1991 and 2003, pushed the distinction between the two to the fore by describing the first as a matter of necessity and the second as a matter of choice.[30] Governments, however, rarely refer to wars of choice. When committing to combat they prefer to insist that they are following some unassailable strategic logic that permitted no alternative, as opposed to encouraging the view that they might as well not have bothered. The most pertinent distinction may lie less in the exercise of choice, as there is always some choice even if the alternative is capitulation, but in the nature of the choice. Is this a situation in which the choice is forced as a result of a potentially existential threat or is engagement optional? One reason why limited war can be a difficult strategic category is that it is used to refer to conflicts where enough is at stake to demand engagement but not so much as to require a total commitment.

The category became popular not because of a focus of conflicts with limited stakes but because of the danger of employing unlimited means when the stakes were high. Its importance lay in the stark contrast to the expectations of total war created by the world wars. Then the full resources of states were pitted against each other in grim struggles for survival, and conflicts were pushed to their extremities. Once nuclear weapons were introduced, this pointed to an absurd and tragic result. Faced with mutual destruction whatever was at stake was unlikely to be worth an all-out confrontation. Any effort to protect interests through the use of armed force would be governed by how far a state was really prepared to go.

The conundrums this created were first thrown into relief during the Korean War of 1950–53. Although this conflict was hardly limited for the people of Korea in its effects or stakes, the US neither extended the war into China nor used nuclear weapons, and in the end accepted an outcome that could be characterized as stalemate rather than victory. Civilian strategists in the 1950s sought to explain why this was a good rather than a bad outcome. The compromise left one half of Korea under Communist rule (where it has remained stuck) but the world intact.[31] If the US was prepared to fight only total war and lacked a capacity for limited war, normally understood as strong regular forces, it would face a dilemma with an incremental Soviet advance. The danger was of "salami tactics," whereby each slice of the salami would appear not to be worth a major conflict, although, cumulatively, the successive slices would eventually turn into the whole.[32]

Limited war capabilities therefore meant being able to respond to challenges in the terms in which they were posed and so dare the enemy to take the risk of taking the war to another and potentially more dangerous level. It was a way of combining tentativeness about resort to major war without abandoning vital interests. This would be the next stage in coercive diplomacy, a move into serious fighting following the initial threats, demonstrative acts, and possibly economic sanctions. The art lay in maximizing gains while minimizing risks. This required that military moves were synchronized with negotiations, bringing the emotional heat of war and the cool calculations necessary to strike a deal into the same space, despite their uneasy coexistence. While employing limited force and constructing credible threats, lines of diplomatic communication must be maintained and demands shaped by priorities rather than vengeance.

With the end of the East-West confrontation, the issue of limited war became less pressing. The wars fought by Western countries were inherently limited. There were challenges in terms of keeping these conflicts restricted in terms of time taken and resources expended, but their discretionary nature meant that if the burdens of a campaign exceeded the value of the objective, then an intervention could be drawn to a close. Forces were always held in reserve. In this respect the conflict between Russia and Ukraine had less in common with the post–Cold War interventions and resembled more past limited wars as neither side committed everything to the conflict.

In a negative sense, limited war as a strategy that refuses to move beyond a certain level of violence (and certainly precludes resort to nuclear weapons) is easy to grasp. In a more positive sense, as a way to achieve objectives rather than always ending up in an impasse, it is more problematic. There are a number of reasons for this.

First, and despite the natural assumption of some proportionality between limited ends and limited means, objectives can shift as a result of the fighting. Threatening armed force creates a new issue in a strategic relationship and an extra source of controversy. Once force has actually been employed, attitudes tend to harden, possibly even obscuring the original cause of the dispute. Governments do not wish to be accused of being "paper tigers," with an appearance of ferocity belied by a practice of timidity.[33] With more violence, compromise becomes harder. Previously acceptable solutions become an insult to those who have died.

Second, as noted with coercive diplomacy, military commitments must reflect the logic of combat. Forces need to be sized by reference to those of the enemy as well as the value of whatever is in dispute. Applying only an amount of military strength proportionate to the stakes involved might risk defeat.

Third, the belligerents need to agree, if only tacitly, not to fight at full capacity. This is different from accepting those natural limits imposed by resources and geography, and also from those circumstances in which a strong state employs only limited forces to deal with opponents with inferior capabilities so that a full victory can be achieved with limited effort. The question with limited war is whether both sides, voluntarily, can accept limits. This requires some means by which limits are recognized, agreed, and enforced, along with some shared understandings about thresholds and boundaries. There might be natural lines—set by geography or types of weaponry or targets—but they may still need to be confirmed through forms of communication and negotiation.

To explain why limited wars may not stay limited, two metaphors have come to be employed: escalators and quagmires. They both warn against complacency when initiating military action on even a modest scale. Both conjure up the image of one thing leading to another, a chain of events that will turn the most restrained first move into an unmitigated disaster. Step on the escalator and you are taken inexorably up the scale of violence until you reach utter calamity. Step into the quagmire and you will soon be bogged down, thrashing about, unable to escape. Of the two concepts, escalation is the better known. Since the early 1960s discussion of any type of conflict, whether industrial, communal, or international, has often had a reference to escalation. To accuse an adversary of escalating is to point to provocative, reckless behavior.

The word "escalation" entered the lexicon during the 1950s to explain why once forces of great size and complexity began to clash, a conflict would become increasingly hard to manage. Actions might be taken because of confusion, misapprehension, panic, and passion. As questions of reputation, credibility, and pride came into play, the military effort might be ratcheted up to levels well beyond those justified by the original dispute. This problem could be aggravated by the rhetoric necessary to mobilize public opinion behind any operation. In the end, limited war implied compromise, and this would always be difficult when the enemy had been described in the darkest terms and the stakes raised to existential levels.

In this way escalation came to describe a tragic process, sustained by one of two possible dynamics. The first was reciprocal action—the tit-for-tat mentality that would mean that if one side upped the ante, the other would surely follow.[34] The second possible dynamic was that of miscalculation, or accident. Everyone involved in war, from the soldier on the ground to the national leader, may be forced to make momentous decisions on the basis of incorrect or inadequate information and misguided intuition. As warfare became more automated, with enormous arsenals controlled by complex systems, the potential impact of such decisions widened. The most disturbing image was of a series of malfunctions setting Armageddon in motion without human intervention—of the end of the world resulting from the flick of the wrong switch. In practice the two were likely to combine. Uncertainty would grow, and so the conflict could become more of a competition in risk-taking. In this way a war could get progressively out of control by degrees.

The escalation metaphor was criticized for failing to recognize the potential for graduated moves, especially during the early stages of a conflict before serious battle was joined. Escalators can go down as well as up. They rarely go straight from the bottom to the top floor. One can get off at some intermediate stages to consider where one is going. In due course the metaphor was stood on its head with the notion of controlled escalation. These theorists of escalation, such as Herman Kahn, suggested that it might be possible to find a level at which a war might be fought that suited one side's capabilities but not the other, posing for the opponent the problem of accepting defeat or moving to yet another, more dangerous level. This was called escalation dominance.[35]

Problems with the idea of controlled or graduated escalation became evident in Vietnam. Here, the Americans hoped to manipulate North Vietnam's behavior through the calibrated use of force, as if steady increments of pain could be added until the enemy's breaking point could be found—the form of coercive diplomacy described by Alexander George as "turn-of-the-screw." The problem here lay in underestimating the enemy's capacity to adjust to steady increases in pressure, and overestimating the extent to which military action could serve as a political signal, especially when it was relied upon to speak for itself without a supporting diplomatic communication. The word "surgical," as used in conjunction with the idea of a "strike," has much to answer for. It conjures up the idea of removing a malignancy yet leaving the healthy parts of an organism unimpaired. As McGeorge Bundy, one of the architects of US policy in Vietnam, pointed out, a surgical military strike "like all surgery, will be *bloody*, messy, and you will have to go back for more."

The failure to coerce the Communists in Vietnam led to a quagmire—a situation in which steady losses were suffered without making evident progress. The precise origins of the quagmire metaphor are obscure. It was implied in those grim pictures of the Western Front, of soldiers stuck in the mire. The sense of being bogged down was as much a description of a physical condition as a telling metaphor. As a depiction of the quandary of a whole nation, as opposed to the lot of a soldier, it seems to have come into circulation after 1945. This was mainly in connection with colonial wars. In relation to Vietnam it was used to describe the French Indochina campaign and was given greatest prominence by the journalist David Halberstam in his Vietnam memoir, *The Making of a Quagmire.*[36]

The metaphor was employed by those who argued that the US had allowed itself to get sucked into an open-ended commitment by optimistic reports from the field to the effect that all that was needed was one more step. The promised victory was never delivered, but in agreeing to each magic "next step " the US became lured deeper and deeper into the morass. This explanation of entanglement was challenged by others. The decisions had been self-conscious, they argued, and the politicians had been warned. The possibility, indeed the probability, of a quagmire had been spelled out in the analyses provided at each point of decision.[37] American policy in Vietnam was actually determined by the rigidity of the political commitment, which made it very difficult to withdraw. The quagmire resulted from a political stake incommensurate with the available military means and, eventually, with the tolerance of the American political system.

The intuitive dangers of escalators and quagmires are probably overstated. This is not to argue that things cannot get out of hand, for reasons quite unconnected with political objectives. There are examples at both micro and macro levels where the "fog of war" has taken its toll. Military operations have a dynamic all their own, and this undermines all attempts to organize them for purposes of political signaling. It is also the case that in total war—when defeat could mean the elimination of the state—the fight may be continued because so much has already been invested, even if this takes it to terrifying levels of violence. The problem is with the suggestion that these processes are independent of political decision. Talk of escalators and quagmires—relentless, independent processes—encourages the view that considered strategic judgments, weighing available military means against desirable political ends, become irrelevant. If military engagements are shaped by the logic of political commitment, then it must be governmental decisions, however flawed and misinformed, that are crucial when it comes to altering the scope and intensity of conflicts. The problem may therefore be one of a growing risk of distortion in political decision making: as conflicts become more complex, the military situation becomes more uncertain, and the political system itself comes under increasing strain.

EXHAUSTION

The classical strategists sought a decisive early battle to bring a war to a quick conclusion before it could become unlimited in the demands placed on manpower and resources. In the absence of a decisive battle, and with a determination to avoid escalation to more dangerous forms of warfare, the question with a limited war was how to bring it to a conclusion. One answer was a political settlement, especially if neither side could see a route to an eventual victory. The other answer was to accept the long haul, find ways to sustain the fight at a level that precluded defeat even if it did not promise an early victory. Rather than risk bold offensives or give up when they have not actually been beaten, they could wait for the opponent to weary of the struggle, or some other development such as support from a new ally.

At the end of the nineteenth century, the German military historian Hans Delbrück suggested such an alternative to the fast and decisive campaign with which the German General Staff was fixated.[38] He distinguished between *Niederwerfungsstrategie*, a strategy of annihilation that would take out the enemy's army leaving the enemy state with no choice but capitulation, and *Ermattungsstrategie*, a strategy of exhaustion by which the ends of war might be achieved by a variety of means including battle, but also forms of economic pressure such as blockade. This was not a means of avoiding battle. It simply acknowledged that battles might not be conclusive on their own. Instead they would have a cumulative effect as part of an effort to wear the enemy down.

Ermattungsstrategie was also translated as a strategy of attrition, and it was attrition that became the more prominent concept. However, its meaning shifted during the course of the twentieth century in the light of the experience of the First World War. During the war's course, attrition as a strategy represented a harsh and remorseless approach to campaign casualties.[39] Because no shortcuts to victory had been found, there appeared to be little choice but to inflict unsustainable losses on the enemy, even though that meant accepting heavy losses of one's own. Victory would go to the side with the most manageable "rate of wastage." A narrower use of the term referred to attempts to weaken enemy forces prior to a coming battle, for example, by pounding forward positions with artillery barrages so that they might then be overwhelmed by an advancing army. This was the idea behind the Battle of the Somme in the summer of 1916 and required careful coordination of shelling and the forward movement of ground forces. Unfortunately this plan left no opportunity to assess the effects of the artillery before the advance began, a flaw that was painfully exposed at the Somme on July 1, 1916.

In either its broader or narrower sense, the idea of attrition never quite escaped association with a wanton tolerance of carnage, a desire to inflict maximum casualties on the enemy for want of an alternative. The strategic theorists of the interwar years sought ways to win wars without mass slaughter by outsmarting the opponent. Advantage should be gained through maneuver so that the enemy was caught by surprise and left disoriented. It was imperative to avoid frontal assaults against a well-prepared enemy. In wars that promised to be long hauls due to the resources of the belligerents, it was best to conserve manpower and not waste it in futile set-piece encounters. This experience, along with that of the Second World War, which was more of a war of movement, demonstrated that attrition was inescapably linked with battle rather than an alternative to battle.

In this way, the distinction between maneuver and attrition developed into one about different ways of fighting. Attrition's reputation as a callous and unimaginative approach to warfare took hold, reinforced in the Korean War after an impasse was reached in 1951,[40] and then again in Vietnam as the US cast around for a way to defeat a persistent opponent. The instinctive approach in Vietnam appeared to be to kill off as many of the enemy forces as possible with superior firepower. The hope was that at some point Communist forces would become ineffective and Hanoi would decide that it could no longer support the southern insurgency. This approach, symbolized by a focus on "body counts," earned the scorn of military reformers in the US after they pulled out from Vietnam. The reformers urged that the US rediscover operational art and damned attrition as an inferior form of strategy, offering maneuver as a far more attractive alternative. This caricatured version of attrition presented it as a warped mindset, marked by a lazy reliance on firepower and the systematic destruction of known targets, sufficiently predictable to be readily countered by a more talented opponent. All this reflected the offensive bias prevalent in classical strategic thought, with its preference for dramatic maneuvers, rapid advances, and knockout blows.

Attrition was left as the orphan of strategy, derided for its tolerance of casualty, its lack of dash and ambition, and its indistinct route to victory. No prominent theorist acted as a champion of attrition and while practitioners often embraced it, this was always grudging. On the rare occasions when it was adopted from the start as a deliberate strategy, the results were unimpressive. An explicit "war of attrition" was launched by the Egyptian leader Gamal Abdel Nasser in March 1969.[41] He believed that the Israelis could not cope if their forces arrayed on one side of the Suez Canal suffered regular casualties as a result of routine shelling. He hoped that as a result they would be persuaded to move away from the Canal area. The Israeli response was to use deep air raids in the hope that this might topple Nasser. This war ended in August 1970 with a cease-fire that saw Israel still in position and Nasser still in power (although he died the next month). The next war launched by Egypt, in October 1973, was much bolder.

Carter Malkasian, a rare student of attrition, argues that it can involve far more than mindless exchanges of firepower but also "in-depth withdrawals, limited ground offensive, frontal assaults, patrolling, careful defensive, scorched-earth tactics, guerrilla warfare, air strikes, artillery firepower, or raids." Successful attritional campaigns work because they wear down the enemy through a protracted, gradual, and piecemeal process. This might end with a battle, when the enemy could no longer cope, but it could also end with a negotiation. Such strategies worked best, he noted, with limited aims.[42]

One possible distinction is between attrition as a strategy based on affecting the opponent's physical state and exhaustion as affecting the opponent's mental state. J. Boone Bartholomees Jr. suggests something along these lines. He construes attrition narrowly as inflicting casualties until an enemy is unable to defend itself, while exhaustion is about eroding the will of the enemy to continue the fight by denying it resources and undermining economic capacity by such means as a blockade.[43] We can therefore describe attrition as the progressive erosion of enemy capacity, which means it can be a consequence of any sustained military engagement. This can weaken an enemy so that it loses battles but, as a second-order consequence, might also undermine political will. By contrast, exhaustion is a strategic effect, marked by a progressive loss of capacity, energy, commitment, and eventually political will. This effect might be caused by attrition but also by other measures designed to stifle economic activity and reduce access to supplies. The Russo-Ukraine conflict was more about exhaustion than attrition.

Bartholomees notes that whether one considers attrition or exhaustion, the stronger side is still likely to prevail. One can see why this might be the case with attrition, in the sense of depleting capacity, because the one with greater capacity should come out on top. Exhaustion is different, which is why this is a strategy favored by an underdog. With inferior resources, the underdog has no interest in regular battle. The interest instead lies in playing for time. The challenge for an irregular force resisting invasion or fighting oppression, for example, is to remain engaged, which may require coping with and absorbing pain. This superior staying power may be the result of having a greater stake in the fight. This is why such campaigns rarely prosper against a stronger side with an even more substantial stake.

In more peripheral areas, irregular forces can develop strategies that exploit familiarity with local conditions and popular feeling to harass the enemy, leaving it susceptible to fatigue, disenchantment, and a growing sense of futility. Success depends on the battles being of endurance and will rather than between armies. The problem lies in how to take advantage of an apparent decline in the enemy's political will to continue with the fight. With attrition, there is an implication of a notional breaking point when the enemy can cope no longer because it has run out of troops or money. Exhaustion accepts that opponents can adjust to pain and hardship so that any turning point may not be sudden or even easy to identify.

A limited war, in which neither side is fighting at full capacity, aggravates this difficulty. A purely attritional strategy cannot be expected to work in such circumstances because neither side will run out of military capacity. They both must seek to prevail within the accepted constraints. This logic points to a bargain to end the conflict, but if a bargain cannot be found and escalation is still eschewed, then nonmilitary factors are likely to become increasingly important. These will include the functioning of the economy and the ability to maintain domestic political support. Strategic advice in such circumstances points to a combination of conserving and building up capacity to stay in the game, while probing for the weak spots in the enemy's position and working out how to exploit them. Satisfaction will come in the form of small gains and an enemy whose losses and pain exceed your own, but it will also be important to pay attention to attitudes and conditions at home as much as to those on the enemy side.

All this helps explain why strategies of exhaustion tend to be default strategies, taken up when stuck in a defensive stance or caught out by a disappointing offensive. They are not going to be advocated by proponents of war, who are much more likely to promise a quick victory and dismiss the possibility of a protracted and miserable hard grind of a conflict. When the first hopes are dashed, strategies of exhaustion are adopted for want of anything better, in the spirit of Churchill's maxim during the Second World War—"keep buggering on." So this is the sort of strategy belligerents stumble into, requiring improvisation, lacking any clear theory of cause and effect, and without an obvious route to victory. Yet the circumstances in which such strategies come to be adopted are quite common, and the difficulties they face in implementation help alert us to some of the messy realities of modern conflict. With the Russo-Ukraine conflict, the interests at stake for both sides provided insufficient motivation to move it into all-out war. Even with the coercive pressures, both had the capacity to last and were able to adapt to the continuing conflict without feeling obliged to accept a resolution on disadvantageous terms.

ACTING STRATEGICALLY

The strategic art does not reside in the ability to formulate a plan at the start of a crisis that will anticipate all contingencies and provide a clear way through to the desired objective. It is very rare that events will unfold as planned as one strategist's art must be pitted against another's. There are always unexpected developments and unintended consequences. Acting strategically requires flexibility and often improvisation, placing close attention to a changing situation, adapting to its new demands, and accepting that outcomes will be different from those wished for at the start. It helps to have a clear sense of the interests at stake and the range of desirable outcomes, as well as the power relationships at the heart of the conflict.

While much writing on strategy concentrates on how to seize initiatives and achieve victories, in this chapter I have emphasized the limits of strategy. These flow from the constraints on any exercise of power, including the risks posed by the opponent's countermeasures and of escalation. The first moves in a conflict may be bold and ambitious, but if they do not succeed quickly, then expectations will need to be scaled back and future moves undertaken with more care. The alternative is to raise the stakes, commit all available resources, and accept the resulting costs, however severe, or at least give a credible impression of being ready to accept all risks. In practice, as this case study will demonstrate, contemporary strategy is more likely to be about finding ways to limit liabilities and risks without conceding on core interests.

The Russia-Ukraine Conflict

ORIGINS

The conflict between Russia and Ukraine erupted on a known fault line in the international system, the result of developments within the states involved but also, more broadly, the shocks to the system resulting from the end of the Cold War, the breakup of the Soviet Union, and the growing activism of NATO countries. It was one of a number of conflicts shaped by a complex relationship between sovereign territory and national identity, often reflected in the secessionist demands faced by multinational states.

The steady disintegration of Yugoslavia affected European politics for most of the 1990s and shaped debates about the proper pursuit of both security and humanitarian concerns. The disintegration was the result of the increasingly nationalist politics of Serbia under the leadership of Slobodan Milosevic. Yugoslavia's constituent republics began to demand independence, starting with Slovenia in June 1991. This was managed largely peacefully, but the secessions of Croatia and Bosnia-Herzegovina led to bloodshed and disruption. The conflict over Kosovo was the most contentious. This was in part because, according to the Yugoslav constitution, it was not a separate republic but a province of Serbia, and also a territory that the Serbs believed to be at the core of its history and identity. The bulk of the population did not see themselves as Serbian. The Kosovar identity was Muslim Albanian. As the Kosovars became more assertive in expressing their national aspirations, the Serbs began to take more drastic measures. This involved repression and intimidation, with the apparent intent of encouraging a mass exodus of Kosovars to neighboring states. In 1998 NATO put pressure on Slobodan Milosevic's government in Belgrade to show restraint. When the conflict erupted again in March 1999, with reports of massacres and expulsions, NATO launched an air campaign. After a tentative start, NATO concluded that a few days of bombing would not make much impression on Serbian resolve. The campaign was therefore stepped up, coming to include attacks directed against targets in Belgrade. Eventually Serbia capitulated, and the refugees were allowed home.[1] This was taken as a rare example of successful coercion through air power although the actual position was more complex with Belgrade facing a growing possibility of serious land warfare and a tough insurgency as the Kosovo Liberation Army gained in strength.

This conflict introduced new rationales for intervention, based on alleviating humanitarian distress and protecting vulnerable minorities. It qualified the principle of noninterference in internal affairs, elevated the principle of self-determination, and reduced the standing of the Security Council, because the threat of a Russia veto meant that NATO acted on its own rationales without seeking authorization for the use of armed force. It was also a key moment in Russia's disenchantment with post–Cold

War security arrangements, and one to which Russian leaders would regularly refer.

Vladimir Putin first came to power as prime minister in 1999. In 2000 he became president, anointed by the ailing Boris Yeltsin. Putin quickly gained a reputation as a tough leader following the suppression of Chechnya secessionists. As he worked to create a more effective Russian state, he benefitted from the revival of the economy as it started to reap the benefits of higher oil and gas prices. From 2000 to 2008 the economy grew at annual rate of 7 percent. Putin saw opportunities to make common cause with the West after the 9/11 attacks on the United States, but then became disillusioned when President Bush and the British prime minister Tony Blair disregarded the norms of international order that they continually claimed to be upholding with their 2003 invasion of Iraq. For Putin this confirmed an impression already created by Kosovo.

At issue was not only whether Western countries considered themselves to be able to act without restraint in an international system in which they enjoyed unprecedented power, but whether Russia's security was threatened as a result. Many post-Communist states joined NATO (Hungary, Poland, and the Czech Republic as the conflict over Kosovo began) and then the European Union. This was largely beneficial to those countries, in terms of governance and economics as well as security, but the trend was viewed from Moscow with increasing misgivings. The idea that the US and its allies ignored rules and commitments when it did not suit them was reinforced by the allegation that NATO had reneged on promises, made as the Cold War ended, not to expand eastward. This became an important part of the Russian narrative, backed by a number of critics of Western policy. Published documents from 1990 do show that verbal assurances were given to Mikhail Gorbachev, the last president of the Soviet Union.[2] These documents were in the context of negotiations over German unification. The unity was either going to be as a neutral state, which was unacceptable to its allies, or as part of NATO. Gorbachev eventually went along with this. At the same time, these documents also demonstrate that Western leaders barely grasped the dynamics of the new situation, including the possibility that the Soviet Union itself would soon fall apart. As this possibility loomed into view, they saw it not as a strategic gain but as a source of disruption and uncertainty.

One example of how the US administration was anxious to help the Soviet Union hold together, even after the fall of the Berlin Wall, was the speech President George H. W. Bush delivered to the Ukrainian Parliament (the Rada) on August 1, 1991, after a meeting with Gorbachev. Bush's objective was to support Gorbachev in his efforts to reform the Soviet system in such a way as to allow for greater autonomy for individual republics while avoiding complete fragmentation. In his speech Bush warned against full independence for Ukraine and refused to meet with nationalist politicians. In a key line he said "Americans will not support those who seek independence in order to replace a far-off tyranny with a local despotism. They will not aid those who promote a suicidal nationalism based upon ethnic hatred." This speech was delivered at a time when bitter fighting had just developed in Yugoslavia between Serbs and Croats. It was criticized by Ukrainian nationalists as a message on behalf of Gorbachev and was nicknamed the "Chicken Kiev" speech by the conservative journalist William Safire for "misreading" history and not embracing democratic movements in the Soviet Union.[3] By the end of the year the Soviet Union had dissolved.

At first NATO sought to meet the demands of post-Communist states for closer association with the alliance through the "Partnership for Peace."[4] This was insufficient to satisfy former Soviet satellites (some with memories of the consequence of appeasement in the 1930s) anxious that they might be gobbled up again without the protection of an alliance. Despite concerns among established NATO members about provoking Moscow and acquiring future liabilities that might be hard to meet, President Clinton in 1994 decided that requests for full membership were reasonable and should be respected. Enlargement did not become a major issue until it began in earnest in the late 1990s, and especially in 2004 with the accession to NATO of the Baltic States, former members of the Soviet Union.[5]

That was also the year of the EU's big bang, when ten states joined the Union, leaving only former Soviet states excluded and emphasizing the attractions of Western institutions for former communist states. The more unhappy Russia became about this process the more it became convinced that past pledges had been dishonored, even though it could not point to any specific promises or binding guarantees. It could see a progressive disinclination to take its security concerns into account combined with a patronizing attitude to Russia as a potential pole of attraction for other former Soviet republics.

In compensation for its general acquiescence in NATO enlargement, Russia was given privileged opportunities for consultation as security issues developed. It was also drawn into high-level international bodies. The Group of Seven leading industrialized nations, for example, became the Group of Eight. A special mechanism was set up to manage the Russian relationship with NATO, with the notional possibility that this could

lead eventually to Russia joining the alliance. But this was all inadequate to cope with the developing situation in Europe as the
interests of Russia and its former satellites diverged. The Baltic
States had been part of the Soviet Union, but this status had never
been recognized by the West because of the way they had been
occupied in 1940 following the Molotov-Ribbentrop pact. While
Albania and Croatia, who joined in 2009, were of marginal interest to Russia, when Georgia and Ukraine, core members of the
old Soviet Union, gradually moved up the agenda, Russia became
alarmed. For these countries to consider joining NATO was tantamount to treachery.

By the time this stage was reached, in 2008, the question was
more pressing for Moscow because the alliance was now seen as
more hostile and indifferent to Russian interests than had been
the case in the 1990s. It was one thing for sovereign states to decide to join NATO. It was another if the regimes of these states
were first changed so that they then became more inclined to join
NATO. This prospect by itself alarmed Putin, but the alarm grew
with the thought that a future revolution might topple him, as
past Russian leaders had been toppled. The first post-Communist
leader to be pushed out by waves of popular protests in the capital city was Serbia's Slobodan Milosevic in 2000. Then came the
"Rose" Revolution in Georgia in 2003 and the 2004 "Orange"
Revolution in Ukraine (followed less convincingly by the
2005 "Tulip" Revolution in Kyrgyzstan). These saw unpopular
and corrupt governments fall in the face of street protests and
demands for reform.[6] Putin was deeply troubled by the possibility
of these revolutions being imitated in Russia, not least because
he was as corrupt as these other leaders even if also more popular.[7] This insecurity led to the strong authoritarian turn in his

approach to domestic politics, with attempts to marginalize and expel opposition politicians and undermine non-governmental organizations (NGOs), especially those with overseas funding. Such organizations, he warned, were not "standing up for people's real interests."[8] In Putin's mind there was a close link between the so-called color revolutions and NATO expansion.[9] A Western-leaning regime was a natural preliminary to membership in NATO, which would then consolidate the new regime's position.

Yet the expansion was demand-led. There were too many precedents from the 1930s and 1940s for these states to be confident that neutrality was a safe option. It was hardly surprising that Russia's neighbors were wary not just of its close interest in its "near abroad," but also by regular assertions of responsibility for Russian-speaking minorities left stranded by the contraction in the Soviet Union's borders. This had already manifested itself well before NATO expansion began in the form of interventions in support of breakaway entities. The precedent was set with Transnistria, a strip of land on Moldova's border with Ukraine, which fought for secession in 1992. The cease-fire agreement left the territory effectively under Russian control and with a garrison of Russian troops. At the same time, South Ossetia declared itself independent of Georgia. There was a similar pattern with Abkhazia: a war against Georgia in 1992–93, which the Georgians lost; an attempt to resolve the conflict, with cease-fire agreements; UN monitoring forces; and a Russian-dominated peacekeeping operation.[10]

Putin expressed his unhappiness with the reshaping of the European security system forcefully in March 2007 in a speech to a largely NATO audience in Munich. The idea of a unipolar world, he told his audience, was pernicious as it allowed the dominant power to show "disdain for the basic principles of international law." NATO expansion represented "a serious provocation," reducing the level of mutual trust. Here he quoted a speech of former NATO general secretary Manfred Wörner of May 17, 1990: "the fact that we are ready not to place a NATO army outside of German territory gives the Soviet Union a firm security guarantee." This was an example of the Russian fixaion on the narrative of NATO betrayal. What Wörner had actually said however was "we are ready not to deploy NATO troops beyond the territory of the Federal Republic," that is into the former East Germany.[11] Though the "stones and concrete blocks of the Berlin Wall have long been distributed as souvenirs," Putin continued, the West was now imposing "new dividing lines and walls on us." Is it possible, he asked, "that we will once again require many years and decades, as well as several generations of politicians, to dissemble and dismantle these new walls?"[12]

Almost immediately the consequences of this new chill began to be felt. In April 2007 there was a row with Estonia. At issue was the removal of a Soviet war monument from the center of Tallin, the capital of Estonia, leading to rioting by members of the country's large ethnic Russian population. As tempers flared, Germany brokered a truce. Russia made its views known through a prolonged cyberattack, which reached a peak on May 9, the anniversary of Germany's defeat in 1945. It targeted government websites, news agencies, and large banks.[13]

The next big issue was Georgia. The Bush administration saw the enlargement of NATO as much about shared values ("the freedom agenda") as about geopolitics. The new members, as well as Russia, were likely to see the security agenda to be of greater importance. This came to a head in April 2008 at a NATO summit in Bucharest. There President George W. Bush raised the possibility of Georgian and Ukrainian membership in the alliance.[14] Angela Merkel of Germany wished to avoid further provoking Russia. She managed to water down the Bucharest declaration so that there was no immediate mechanism (Membership Action Plan) for the two countries to join the alliance. Yet the declaration stated starkly that "we agreed today that these countries will become members of NATO."[15] As a compromise this was the worst of both worlds: no enlargement would actually take place but the firm statement of intent was provocative. Putin, who was present for the last day of the summit, picked up on the provocation: "We view the appearance of a powerful military bloc on our borders . . . as a direct threat to the security of our country."[16]

The president of Georgia, Mikhail Saakashvili, despite being urged to tread carefully, decided that this was a good moment to push back against the Ossetian separatists. A combination of heightened tensions aggravated by misapprehensions led in August 2008 to a Georgian military offensive. The aim was to reclaim territory. The result was that Ossetian forces, greatly assisted by Russians, gained full control.[17] The somewhat chaotic Russian response to the initial Georgian moves, which at first left the South Ossetians coping on their own, does not suggest that this was a Russian setup. This seems also to have been the view in Western capitals, despite denunciations of Russian aggression.[18]

The precedent cited by the Russians for this action was Kosovo, not only because it had been given military support by NATO in 1999 to separate from Serbia but also because it had declared its full independence in February 2008. Dmitry Medvedev, then president of Russia, argued that he could not say to "the Abkhazians and Ossetians (and dozens of other groups around the world) that what was good for the Kosovo Albanians was not good for them. In international relations, you cannot have one rule for some and another rule for others."[19]

Medvedev was president because the Russian constitution required that Putin stand down after two terms. Putin had kept his influence by putting Medvedev, who had run his presidential administration, into the position. Putin then became prime minister. In the West, there was hope that Medvedev would be more of a moderate—and more of a modernizer—than Putin. When President Obama came to office at the start of 2009, he sought a "reset" in relations with Russia.[20] There was little follow-up after the invasion of Georgia, although this was largely because of the pressing demands of the financial crisis that began soon after. Michael McFaul, Obama's ambassador to Moscow, describes the Medvedev years as being warmer, noting a new Strategic Arms Reduction Treaty, cooperation over sanctions on Iran on its nuclear program and the fight against the Taliban in Afghanistan, support for Russia to join the World Trade Organization, and tension avoided when President Bakiev of Kyrgyzstan was toppled in 2010.[21] When Medvedev met Obama in March 2012 in Seoul he observed, "[W]e probably enjoyed the best level of relations between the United States and Russia during these three years than ever during the previous decades."[22]

In October 2011 Medvedev failed to veto a Security Council resolution that eventually led to the fall of the Libyan leader Colonel Muammar Gaddafi. Putin believed this was an error, confirmed by what he took to be another example of the West's double-dealing. As he saw it, the UN mandate was overinterpreted by the Western countries, taking it from a humanitarian mission to prevent a massacre of rebels in the city of Benghazi to support for the rebels in subsequent regime change. Having messed up its intervention in Iraq, it was now doing the same in Libya, thus allowing an anarchic situation to develop, which allowed radical Islamists to take advantage. Yet another long-standing opponent of the West was not only overthrown but also murdered, resulting in a previously stable country being engulfed in chaos.

Putin's irritation with this move was combined with a fear that he was next in line. In late 2011 he announced that he would stand again for president and that Medvedev would become prime minister. This led to mass anti-Putin demonstrations in Moscow and elsewhere.[23] The demonstrators alleged that Putin was rigging the parliamentary elections, a claim familiar from the previous color revolutions and, in this case, with some foundation. There was evidence of ballot boxes being stuffed with fake votes.[24] In December, US secretary of state Hillary Clinton expressed "serious concerns about the conduct of the election" and called for a "full investigation."[25] The protests never reached the scale of the other color revolutions, and the dissent was put down ruthlessly.

The episode reinforced Putin's conviction that the regime could not take its apparently unassailable political position for granted, and that the US government was determined to use popular protests to topple any government, however legitimate, that it did not like. The Kremlin claimed that American assistance went beyond verbal support to funding.[26] From now on relations were much cooler. Obama did not invite Putin to the NATO summit in 2012 and signed into law the Magnitsky Act (to which he had originally objected). This put sanctions on Russian tax officials and police involved in a scam, which had led to Sergei Magnitsky, a lawyer, being put in prison, where he died.[27] When he went to the G20 summit in St. Petersburg in September 2013,

Obama met with human rights activists. On the eve of the Ukraine crisis, therefore, US-Russian relations were already deteriorating, with the Americans objecting to human rights abuses and Putin fearing that they wished his overthrow. Putin's new presidency had a harsher face than before, playing to a conservative audience that was homophobic, xenophobic, and nationalist.

EUROPEAN UNION VS. EURASIAN UNION

Ukraine is a large country in the middle of Eastern Europe, neighbors to Poland, Hungary, Slovakia, Romania, Moldova, and Belarus, as well as Russia, with a population of some 45 million.[28] The territory has long been contested, and its history is one of regular fragmentation and unsettled borders, with the western and eastern parts often separated. The area north of the Black Sea, sometimes known as "Novorossiya," with Odessa to the south, Kharkiv to the north, and Donetsk to the east was taken from the Ottoman Empire in the eighteenth century and colonized aggressively by Catherine the Great. During the nineteenth century a Ukrainian nationalist movement took root. As a result of the short-lived Brest-Litovsk Treaty of 1918 between Russia and Germany, Ukraine gained independence. Its borders were then contested after the end of the Great War. After 1919, Western Ukraine, which had not been part of the Russian Empire, was divided up among a number of countries, although most of it was incorporated into Poland. It was then joined with the rest of Ukraine following the Soviet Union's invasion in 1939—and then again after the German forces that had invaded in 1941 were expelled in 1945. Nikita Khrushchev, who eventually took power after Stalin's death in 1953, sought to improve Russian-Ukrainian relations (he had served as first secretary of the Ukrainian Soviet Socialist Republic from 1948 to 1949). In 1954 he arranged for Crimea, which had been in Russia, to be transferred to Ukraine. The best explanation for the move, which did not go down well in Crimea, was that Khrushchev was boosting the role of the Ukrainian party bosses to get their support in the post-Stalin power struggle which had yet to be concluded.[29] Soviet Ukraine "was designed in Moscow from territories conquered and controlled by the Red armies" with "little consideration of local sentiment or the coherence and legitimacy of the resultant polities."[30]

In addition to these shifting borders, three intense tragedies influenced Ukrainian-Russian relations. The first was the "great famine" of 1932–33, known as the Holodomor ("extermination through hunger"), when some 3.9 million Ukrainians starved to death. This was the time of the Soviet leader Joseph Stalin's policy of forced collectivization of agriculture. The Holodomor was not just the tragic result of a bad policy but deliberate as food was confiscated from the Ukrainians. Hence the allegation of "genocide."[31] Starvation was used as a form of class warfare against peasants, coercing them to joining collective farms. Second, and linked, was the Stalinist terror during which—in addition to those presumed hostile to the Soviet leadership who were purged, exiled, and executed—were added those who had supported Ukrainian independence in the past or might do so in the future. The next great tragedy was the Second World War. Despite the strong anti-Soviet sentiment, which led to some nationalists fighting alongside the Germans, Nazi brutality left most Ukrainians with little choice but to join the Soviet effort to resist the occupation and push out the invaders. Ukraine suffered disproportionately, losing up to 8 million people during the war. Less than a fifth of these were in the military. The war left infrastructure wrecked, and this was followed by yet more famine.

As one of the largest republics and with its leadership fully Sovietized after the purges, Ukraine was integrated into the Soviet Union. It was the location for vital defense industries and military facilities. Many Ukrainians held important positions. Yet still a distinctive Ukraine national identity developed over time, with its own political culture, and was recognized by Ukrainian communists. As soon as it became clear that the Soviet Union was headed for dissolution, Ukraine asserted its sovereignty. On December 1, 1991, three weeks before the demise of the Soviet Union, the Ukrainian people supported independence in a referendum (by 90 percent) and elected the chairman of parliament, Leonid Kravchuk, as the first president. The new freedom was not matched by new prosperity. There was a major economic slowdown as Ukraine struggled to adjust to a harsh new environment. This led to growing popular discontent, focused not only on a decline in living standards but also the growing corruption among the elite. Although Ukraine's economic position improved from the late 1990s, there was still discontent, with corruption always a major theme.

The corruption was exemplified by Viktor Yanukovych, a key figure in this story. He was born in Dontesk in 1950 and became its governor in 1997. He used every opportunity to acquire wealth and secure his power base. In 2002 Kravchuk appointed him prime minister and then chose him as his successor as president. He would be sufficiently weak to allow Kravchuk continuing influence, while maintaining the established policy of staying close to Russia and exploring improved links with the West. For that reason he was also Putin's candidate. Putin tried to help his election by easing restrictions on Ukrainian migrant workers, reducing energy prices, and giving interviews with the Ukrainian media in which he stressed the shared heritage of the two countries. Yanukovych, however, was caught out by a strong campaign by the opposition leader Viktor Yushchenko, an economist who had been chairman of the National Bank. While this was underway, Yushchenko was mysteriously and almost fatally poisoned, with Moscow—not unreasonably—the main suspect.[32] In the second ballot Yanukovych scraped home, but the suspicion that this was rigged led to massive street demonstrations and the "Orange Revolution." The demonstrators protested the manipulation of the political process by remnants of the old order, still attached to Communist ways and to Russia. There were also accusations in the other direction arguing that Western individuals and groups had helped the activists with money and training.

This led to fresh elections, which brought Yushchenko to power. Yulia Tymoshenko, a businesswoman with knowledge of the energy field, became prime minister, and Petro Poroshenko, a businessman who owned Roshen chocolates, had the defense and security portfolio. Yushchenko's presidency was chaotic, not helped by his continuing physical weakness. After a year he dismissed both Tymoshenko and Poroshenko. Ukrainian politics were now dominated by the complex interactions between these figures and Yanukovych, all of which was complicated further by the painful negotiations with Russia about how much should be paid for gas supplies. After elections in autumn 2007 in which Tymoshenko's party did well, she became prime minister once again, but Yushchenko was still suspicious of her. Relations between the two broke down again. More turmoil followed the 2008 financial crash and disputes with Russia over energy prices. With his rivals in disarray, Yanukovych crept back into power in the 2010 election. Now he sought to strengthen his position by pushing for a quasi-presidential system, as Parliament had gained more say after the 2004 revolution. He also put Tymoshenko on trial for embezzlement, leading to a sentence of seven years imprisonment.

Putin was at first relatively relaxed about the "Orange" leadership and not too worried about its overtures to the EU. At that time Russia's own links with the EU were quite strong. Over time the relationship soured, especially over energy prices, and Putin was strongly opposed to the idea that Ukraine might join NATO. When Yanukovych came to power, relations improved and NATO membership was off the table.[33] Yanukovych also found himself under intense pressure from Russia to sign a range of cooperation agreements. He met with Medvedev seven times in his first 100 days in office.[34] But the EU issue was still live. Yanukovych was aware that a successful negotiation with Brussels would be very popular and help secure his reelection.

The success of countries that had joined the EU encouraged those in Ukraine who wanted to follow a similar path. The integration of former Central and East European countries into the EU had a transformational effect on their economies. The comparisons between Poland and Ukraine were instructive, for both had developed in similar ways under Communist rule. Their fates since then had been wildly divergent. Between 1990 and 2012 Ukraine's economy had shrunk by more than 30 percent while Poland's had doubled in size, so that Polish per capita incomes were five times those of Ukrainians.[35] For those stuck in the corrupt, subsidized, heavy-industry stagnation of post-Communism, association with the EU offered a path to prosperity they were unlikely to find elsewhere.

By 2013, however, the implications of getting close to the EU had changed. Following the 2004 big bang, EU expansion had reached the borders of the former Soviet Union, and had already taken in the Baltic states. The fact that an Association Agreement with Ukraine was even on the table was the result of an initiative taken by those EU countries closest to Russia, most with experience of being in the Soviet sphere of influence. They sought ways to assist those who had yet to join Western institutions but were clearly wary of Russian pressure. This resulted in the EU's Eastern Partnership. This was a series of summits involving EU states with Armenia, Azerbaijan, Belarus, Georgia, Moldova, and Ukraine. The first was in Prague in summer 2009 and the second in Warsaw in September 2011. The goal was described as "building a common area of democracy, prosperity, stability, and increased interactions and exchanges." Major political and socioeconomic reforms were required of the partner countries. An Association Agreement would involve Deep and Comprehensive Free Trade Agreements (DCFTAs). In return for the reduction of barriers to trade with the EU there must be consolidation of democratic institutions, protection of human rights, promotion of a market economy, and gradual adoption of EU rules and regulations. If they could be achieved, then the prospect was one of progressive "economic integration in the EU Internal Market, and therefore to the creation of an economic area between the EU and partner countries."[36]

Putin had appeared less concerned about these countries getting closer to the EU than could ever be the case with NATO.

As the demanding nature of the Association Agreements became clear, the concern grew. "We are accused of having spheres of influence," observed Foreign Minister Sergie Lavrov, "but what is the Eastern Partnership, if not an attempt to extend the EU's sphere of influence, including to Belarus?"[37] And Russia was still interested in its own sphere. Putin wished to find a way to pull the Soviet Union's component parts back together, even if it could not be re-created as a state. Not long after the Warsaw summit of the Eastern Partnership, Russia announced on November 18, 2011, an agreement with Kazakhstan and Belarus (which because of its human rights record was something of an outlier in the Eastern Partnership) to establish a Eurasian Customs Union (ECU) by 2015.[38] (It was later renamed the Eurasian Economic Union, EEU). This was to mimic the EU both in terms of starting as a customs union and then becoming something more—a supranational entity (obviously dominated by Russia) that would bring together economies, legal systems, customs services, and even military capabilities to rival the EU, the US, and China.

Whether this aspiration was ever realistic, it nonetheless had evident attractions to Putin. His efforts to modernize the Russian economy so that it could interact more effectively with the West had failed. For a leader who saw the collapse of the Soviet Union as "a major geopolitical disaster of the century,"[39] this was the only chance to begin a partial reconstruction, even if it meant interacting largely with economies with similar pathologies to Russia's own. The discontent he witnessed in late 2011 in Moscow had reinforced his determination to strengthen the state apparatus. Against this backdrop, the ECU appeared as almost the last option for a transnational context in which Russian power could be exercised. Previous efforts to establish institutions which could combine Russian hegemony with practical cooperation—the Commonwealth of Independent States and the Single Economic Space—had yielded little.

The inclusion of only Belarus and Kazakhstan would not, however, be sufficient. To make this work, Armenia, Moldova, and Ukraine were also required. Of these, Ukraine was the most essential for it was a large country and so much a part of the Russian past. Yet in the coming summit, scheduled for Vilnius in November 2013, in the series organized under the aegis of the EU Eastern Partnership, these three countries would be invited to sign Association Agreements with the EU, covering trade. Putin's plan risked frustration.

Armenia, Moldova, and Ukraine had to be stopped from slip- ping away into the Western sphere. A campaign was soon un- derway directed at these countries to prevent them from moving toward the EU.[40] This even included measures taken against Lithuania, now a member of the EU and the host of the November summit, with bans on imports of its dairy products into Russia. Armenia, isolated and dependent upon Russia, made little effort to resist and in early September walked away from the EU to- ward the ECU. Moldova was put under intense pressure, with references to the contested position of Transnistria.[41] Moldova, Europe's poorest country, was dependent on its wine exports but found these embargoed by Russia (this had happened earlier in spring 2006). Yet Moldova still signed up with the EU in Vilnius. With Ukraine, however, the pressure succeeded. When he had signed up for the Eastern Partnership and taken the first steps to an Association Agreement in 2011, Yanukovych had looked for a compromise formula but this had been rejected out of hand, and he had been told by Moscow that his only option was full cooperation with the ECU.[42] When the moment of choice came in November 2013, Yanukovych announced at the last moment that he was unable to sign the Association Agreement.

This was the result of some ruthles seconomic coercion, in a way that had become almost routine for Russia whenever it needed to influence countries in its neighborhood. There were regular uses of import bans to disrupt trade. Among the targets over the previous couple of decades, in which extra charges and tariffs had been imposed to gain compliance with Russian demands, had been Finland and Sweden (an additional export tax on timber), Poland (meat and vegetables embargo), Estonia (rail tariffs and traffic embargo), and Latvia (rail tariffs).[43] During the 1990s this strategy had some success. Russia adopted such tactics on 39 occasions between 1992 and 1997 and got significant concessions in more than a third of the cases.[44] One of the features of this strategy was that Russian intentions, however transparent, were rarely made explicit. Instead they were explained by "ludicrous cover stories for public consumption."[45] All this relied upon the targets understanding what was expected of them, which they often did, while having the advantage for Moscow that the measures could be quietly dropped if they were not succeeding without evident loss of face. Barely credible cover stories became embedded, not only as a feature of economic coercion or as a way of dealing with domestic opponents (who were often found to be guilty of "tax irregularities"), but as a way of deflecting any criticisms in the international arena.

The energy sector had a special place in this strategy. Energy exports were vital to the Russian economy, making possible a rising standard of living for the Russian people and improvements to military capabilities. In addition, abundant reserves of oil and gas potentially offered a form of power, compensating for a decline in other forms. The idea that Russia could become an "energy superpower" had been around since the mid-1990s. During the 2000s Putin settled on this as a "big idea." It did not require creating either a new capability or mythology. "If you have strong legs, you should go into long-jump and not play chess."[46] It did require turning the energy companies into instruments of state policy. This meant reversing the past privatization of energy assets, for example by carving up the private energy firm Yukos, and turning Gazprom and Rosneft into national champions.[47] The idea also benefitted from high energy prices. This is what Russia was enjoying in the mid-2000s when Putin embraced the idea. The country's energy strategy explicitly had as one of its purposes "to promote foreign policy positions."[48]

The deals undertaken by Gazprom, responsible for everything from the extraction to the processing to the distribution and sale of Russian natural gas, came to be shaped by political as well as market conditions. A tight market and few alternative sources of supply created leverage. These deals, in which Putin took a close interest, could offer favors to prized customers and then coerce those considered hostile or ungrateful. As early as 2007, fifty-five instances of Russian attempts to use energy blackmail for political ends had been identified.[49] Even before the end of the Soviet Union, Moscow interrupted oil supplies to the Baltic region in 1990 to try to crush the budding independence movements. It did something similar in 1998 and 1999 with supplies of crude oil to the refinery in Lithuania cut during a contest between Russia and the US to acquire a stake in the refinery.[50] There were disputes with Belarus in 2006 and 2010, and gas was cut off to the Czech Republic when it supported US missile defense plans in 2008.

When the EU finally got details of the price paid by member countries for Russian gas in 2013, the range was too great to be explained by market and distribution factors, and it clearly reflected a system of rewards and punishments. The dependence of European countries on Russian natural gas therefore offered a means of making serious money while also reminding these countries where their interests lay at times of trouble. To strengthen Russian's market position, two ambitious pipeline plans were developed, each with their own winners and losers. North Stream would be a pipeline under the Baltic Sea, built by German companies with Gazprom, cutting out Poland and Belarus who would then lose transit revenue. Its sister project was South Stream, passing through Bulgaria, Greece, and Serbia to Italy and then terminating in France. Both would bypass Ukraine. In addition to the anxieties of the more Russia-phobic countries in Europe about dependence on Moscow, a serious problem for the South Stream project was that it required exceptions from the EU's energy and competition policies if the deals with Hungary and Bulgaria were to go ahead. Despite lobbying from these countries the European Commission was reluctant to agree.[51]

Ukraine was a regular target. As early as 1993 gas had been cut off when discussions were underway with President Kuchma about allowing Russia to retain most of the Black Sea naval fleet. In late 2005, after the Orange Revolution, Russia sought to raise the price of its gas to Ukraine to levels generally considered exorbitant, combined with warnings that the tap could be turned off at any time. Russia reminded its European partners that they too would suffer gas shortages should Russia cut Ukraine's supplies. On January 1, 2006, Russia dropped the pressure in the pipes, and gas deliveries to Austria, Slovakia, and Hungary fell.

Ukraine quickly caved in. The episode had the advantage to Putin of demonstrating to European countries that they depended on Russia to keep the lights on and how Ukraine was a weak and unreliable link in their supply chain. By the same token it also looked like extortion and showed how Russia might threaten rather than guarantee energy security. In January 2009 the same thing happened again in a dispute about how much Ukraine should pay for its gas, and this time the stoppage went on for three weeks.

All this provides the backdrop for Putin's decision in the summer of 2013 to force Ukraine to opt for the ECU instead of the EU. It was a relatively easy target, with a number of forms of pressure available. Yanukovych was personally vulnerable to blackmail because of his highly organized corruption. In addition, the possibility of Crimea's annexation may have been raised. According to Radek Sikorski, the former Polish foreign minister, Polish intelligence became aware of Russian calculations on "what provinces would be profitable to grab."[52] The most effective weapon, however, was trade. Almost a quarter of Ukraine's exports were to Russia. New Russian customs regulations in August 2013 led to restrictions on goods from Ukraine. This caused significant drops in industrial production and exports, and a worsening financial position. The targets were heavy industries that depended on the Russian market and were often located in Eastern Ukraine, and pro-EU businesses, such as Poroshenko's Roshen chocolate (banned for "toxic impurities"). Poroshenko strongly supported closer ties with the EU.

Russia claimed that this was not about putting pressure on Ukraine but was merely an effort to protect its businesses from an influx of cheap European goods through Ukraine. The effect of the Russian move was captured by the ratings agency, Moody's, which almost immediately cut Ukraine's debt rating to C grade. The proposed EU deal was "credit positive in the medium-term, given that it will support Ukraine's institutions." Unfortunately, Moody's went on to observe, "the short-term impact of a negative reaction by Russia outweighs these benefits."

Putin saw the conflict in zero-sum terms, and to some extent so did the EU. Ukraine was being asked to choose between two structures which, in terms of their rules and practices, were incompatible. But neither option was really mature: Ukraine had a long way to go before being able to turn an Association Agreement with the EU into full membership, while the ECU was at most a work in progress. It is arguable that both the EU and Russia were unwise to demand that Ukraine choose between them when the country was so polarized and any choice was unlikely to be definitive. For Putin there is an extra puzzle as to why he was prepared to put so much stress on the individual who was the most sympathetic to Russian interests that he was likely to find in Kiev. Yanukovych's position meant that he was vulnerable to bullying by Putin, but the spectacle of bullying was bound to weaken him further.

As anticipated, Ukraine was pushed close to financial collapse. As the economy contracted by 1.5 percent in the third quarter, foreign reserves fell by 30 percent, and total foreign debt rose to 77 percent of GDP. There was no obvious way of repaying or rolling over some $10.8 billion of foreign debt. After Yanukovych had pulled away from the EU in November, he agreed with Putin in December to a Ukrainian-Russian Action plan. Russia agreed to buy $15 billion of Ukrainian Eurobonds and to reduce the price of Russian natural gas from more than $400 per 1,000 cubic meters to $268.[53] Prime Minister Mykola Azarov explained: "We made such a decision when it became clear that if we sign the agreement [with the EU], we will face crisis. It was absolutely clear and I can answer for that. So we had nothing left to do but change our mind and find other forms of support for Ukraine."[54] The only alternative source of funds for Ukraine was the International Monetary Fund (IMF). The IMF would not help unless Yanukovych agreed to structural economic reforms and "exchange rate flexibility" (i.e., devaluation). A past failure to take such steps had led to a suspension of a $15 billion standby credit in 2011. Now the demands included a major rise in gas bills, a salary freeze, big budget cuts, and lower energy subsidies. The IMF offer was essentially to provide sufficient funds to pay back what was already owed to the Fund in return for a reform program that would reduce the risks of it having to do so again. These terms, presented in a letter on November 20 were, according to Azarov, "harsh." This was the "last straw."[55] Christine Lagarde of the IMF later noted that without a lifeline from Russia "Ukraine was heading nowhere."[56]

Neither the EU nor the IMF was in a position to respond in kind to the Russian offer. Ukraine was not viewed as a great prize for which it was worth making extraordinary efforts.[57] Nor did the EU consider itself to be in competition with the ECU, an organization which it had never taken particularly seriously. There was no attempt to enter into a bidding war with Russia by seeking to match or even exceed the generous terms of the promised Russian loan. After the disappointing aftermath of the Orange Revolution, the EU remained cautious in its dealings with Kiev, with a low opinion of the Ukrainian government and skepticism when given promises of reform. Nor would extra financial assistance have done much good, given the underlying state of

Ukraine's political economy and corruption. In 2013 Ukraine came in 144th out of the 176 countries ranked in the Transparency International Corruption Perceptions Index, in an even worse position than Russia, which was 127th.[58]

In terms of human rights the EU was not especially hard on Ukraine given its poor record of internal governance. It had, however, focused on actions taken against opposition leaders, especially former premier Yulia Tymoshenko, who was in prison. Germany had demanded her release as condition for any EU deal. Yanukovych was reluctant to comply as he still saw her as a threat. When the EU saw a deal with Ukraine slipping away they were even prepared to relax this demand as well.

The EU had been caught napping. As with many crises the form it would take could not be predicted, but the Commission had been too sanguine about the ability of any Yanukovych led government to meet the conditions required by the Association Agreement, or the extent of popular anger at high-level corruption. With Syria providing a major distraction during the second half of 2013 it saw no advantage in picking a fight with Moscow, and therefore tended to ignore the fights that Putin was already picking with Russia's neighbors. It therefore only belatedly appreciated Yanukovych's dilemma, and responded inadequately. It was widely seen to have been defeated by Putin's display of effective coercion. The reaction of many in Brussels was that a closer relationship with Russia, even with the bribe of a large loan, provided no long-term relief for Ukraine. All that the EU could now do, however, was to leave it to Yanukovych to find this out for himself, to "stew in his own juice." One official was quoted as saying: "Six months down the line, when left alone to deal with Russian pressure, he will come to us on his knees."[59]

EUROMAIDAN

As it turned out, the EU and the IMF were back in Kiev within four months. The failure to sign the Association Agreement with the EU and this conspicuous move into the Russian sphere of influence triggered a crisis in Ukraine. There was a sharp public reaction, leading almost immediately to the occupation by numerous protestors of the Maidan Nezalezhnosti (Independence Square), thereby giving the revolution its name, Euromaidan (initially a hashtag on Twitter). It began on November 24, 2013, days after Yanukovych walked away from the EU. The demonstrations were massive and persistent; government offices were taken over and occupied. They were replicated in other cities, largely but not solely in Central and Western Ukraine. Police and security forces tried ineffectually to contain the uprising. Without their efforts it might have petered out on its own accord. The first use of the Berkut (Ukrainian special police) was on November 30 in an attempt to disperse the protestors. By early December the government appealed to the media to limit coverage of the protest. Yanukovych met with Putin at Sochi on December 6 and signed some limited agreements on cooperation. The opposition leader, Arseniy Yatseniuk, claimed that the plan was to sign up with the ECU at the next scheduled meeting on December 17.[60] After the two men met, Putin denied that this was even discussed. In practice for the Russian leader stopping Ukraine associating with the EU was more important than getting it to join the ECU. The two men did agree the $15 billion loan and reduced gas prices. Putin underlined the political implications for Ukraine when he described it as being "without doubt, in the full sense of the word, our strategic partner and ally."[61]

This deal only added urgency to the protests, and they continued into 2014. On January 8, Yanukovych appears to have met Putin secretly in Valdai.[62] This was followed, on January 16, by hurriedly passed laws which criminalized the protests. These led to expressions of international concern, even larger demonstrations, and, as the police tried to enforce the laws, serious violence with the first deaths. This was the moment when Far Right groups brought their weapons to the protests. As the crisis escalated, Yanukovych held talks with opposition figures and offered to bring them into the government, among other concessions. These talks went nowhere and the situation got progressively out of control, with more violent episodes and rumors of provocations on both sides. On February 18, twenty-six people, including ten police officers, lost their lives in clashes between police and demonstrators. Two days later, forty-four demonstrators and three police officers were killed as shots rang out around Maidan Nezalezhnosti.[63] The next day French, German, Polish, and Russian foreign ministers brokered a deal between the opposition and the government that would lead to the restoration of the 2004 constitution, the formation of a national unity government, and new elections by the end of the year.[64] The demonstrators were unimpressed with any deal that allowed Yanukovych to stay. With no sign that the protests would calm down, and with the disappearance of the riot police that had been guarding the presidential compound, he decided not to fight for his position. He fled, despite being told by Putin to stay put.

As with all such uprisings there were questions of legitimacy. How representative were the demonstrators? Was the revolution about what they said it was about or was there a hidden agenda?

Can any government coming into power in such circumstances be considered legitimate? The answer to these questions is important not only in terms of assigning responsibility for this set of events but because it shaped the narrative about what was at stake in the subsequent conflict. From the start Russia insisted that Euromaidan was an instrument of Western policy and supported by hard-line fascist groups. As Yanukovych was the elected president, any successor government was bound to be illegal.

The evidence suggests that the country was divided on Euromaidan, with support high in Central and Western Ukraine and among the young. Polls prior to Yanukovych's switch away from the EU in November had shown support for an Association Agreement three times higher than for one with the Eurasian Customs Union, and on this core issue the protest had public opinion behind it.[65] Their methods were questioned though and there were grave misgivings from the start in the Russophone East.[66] The question of the movement's ideology was complicated by the tendency in Moscow's propaganda to label all groups opposed to Russia, irrespective of their actual ideologies, Nazis or Fascists, because these had been their enemies during the Great Patriotic War.

Euromaidan was supported by a range of political viewpoints. The bulk of those present were appalled not only by the eastward shift in Ukraine's political orientation but also the degree of corruption this would breed in the future. Joining the EU was hardly a right-wing cause. Yet extreme nationalists were present, including members of the so-called Right Sector. In Russian propaganda the specter of Stepan Bandera loomed large. He was the nationalist Ukrainian leader who saw the 1941 German invasion of the Soviet Union as an opportunity to gain independence.

Bandera's Organization of Ukrainian Nationalists (OUN) had fascistic and anti-Semitic aspects, some of which were carried into the Maidan Nezalezhnosti. As opinion began to polarize, their slogans carried extra weight. Some also carried weapons, and so they played their part in the movement taking a violent turn.[67] These activists, however, were never more than a small minority and played only a limited political role in the aftermath.[68] The origins of the violence lay in the government's attempt to suppress the protests by forceful means from the start.

Equally the role of Western governments and institutions can be exaggerated. The EU was always going to look warmly at a political movement that viewed it so positively, but hundreds of thousands of people took to the streets before European politicians came to offer their symbolic support. There were sufficient prompts for protest without Western countries manufacturing them.

In early February the Russians released a taped phone call between Victoria Nuland, a senior State Department official, and Geoffrey Pyatt, the US ambassador to Ukraine. On the tape the two discuss which Ukrainian opposition leaders to try to bring into the government. This is in the context of trying to broker a deal with Yanukovych rather than overthrow him (at one point they discuss "outreach" to him). For Nuland the most embarrassing part of the tape, for which she had to apologize, was when she used an expletive when expressing her exasperation with the pace of EU diplomacy.[69] In the end it was three foreign ministers from EU countries—France, Germany, and Poland—who drafted the agreement of February 21, which was stillborn. Last, while any transfer of political power in such circumstances must be of questionable legality, there was a degree of constitutionality.

Not only did Yanukovych flee but so did many of his party in the Ukrainian Parliament (Rada), which meant that a new government could be sworn in by a majority vote.

The main explanation for the success of Euromaidan can be found in Yanukovych. Even in a system known to be corrupt he was an extreme case, and his focus on his own wealth was well understood from early in his political career, including by Kravchuk and Putin. Putin never held him in high regard, as could be seen in the way that he bullied him conspicuously and effectively in late 2013, helping to create the conditions for the uprising. There was barely any pretense that Yanukovych was making the key judgments on his own volition. He never found ways to address the protests in a constructive fashion and lacked the conviction to crush them ruthlessly. As Shaun Walker put it:

> Yanukovych was a useless democrat; he was also a useless autocrat. He specialized in crackdowns that were brutal enough to radicalize more Ukrainians into action, but not brutal enough to subdue the revolutionary impulses with fear. He was held in contempt by Western leaders for his undemocratic impulses, and by Moscow for his unwillingness to take them far enough.[70]

He did not stand up to the crowds but left the scene, taking what he could of his loot with him. On February 22, as he broadcast a message complaining about "gangsterism, vandalism, and a coup d'état," demonstrators and journalists were wandering around his private estate at Mezhiyhirya, just outside Kiev, where they found vintage automobiles, a private zoo, and even a mock Spanish galleon moored in a lake.[71]

On March 4, 2014, Vitaly Churkin, Russia's permanent representative to the United Nations, presented a copy of a letter signed by Yanukovych, dated March 1, 2014, asking that Putin use Russian armed forces to "restore the rule of law, peace, order, stability and protection of the population of Ukraine." The United States and the European Union were accused of conniving in his illegal overthrow.[72] But the circumstances of his departure meant that his words had no authority, and he could not serve as a rallying figure even for those opposed to what had happened. Yanukovych's weak reputation and subsequent absence meant that those opposed to the new government in Kiev lacked any strong and authentic political figure around whom they could rally.

CRIMEA

While Russia had no intention of invading Ukraine directly to restore the old order, such a rebuff to Putin and his policies could not be ignored. It denounced the new government in Kiev as illegal. Later, the Russian foreign minister, Sergey Lavrov, explained why there had to be a Russian response:

> Would it be acceptable for Russia, considering its international standing, to keep mum and recognize the coup in Ukraine, and to leave Russians and Russian speakers in Ukraine in the lurch after the first order issued by the organizers of the anti-constitutional armed revolt, which was supported by their foreign sponsors, and banned many things that were connected with the Russian language?[1]

Here he referred to a vote in the Ukrainian parliament to make Ukrainian the sole state language at all levels. The vote, taken on February 23, was to repeal a controversial 2012 law, promoted by Yanukovych's Party of Regions. It gave Russian, and other minority languages, the status of "regional languages" Its passing had led to fistfights in Parliament, as opponents claimed it undermined Ukrainian as the language of the nation. Without this law the actual use of these languages would still be protected under the Ukrainian constitution. Nonetheless, the move to repeal coming so soon after Yanukovych's flight caused a strong adverse reaction in Crimea and Russian-speaking areas in Southern and Eastern Ukraine, prompting street protests. The acting president Oleksandr Turchynov, however, vetoed the bill on March 1, arguing the need for a new language law to accommodate all interests. Arguably by this time the initial damage was done, for Russia was already on its way to taking Crimea.

Lavrov's statement suggested urgency. There was no suggestion that any consideration was given to waiting to see whether Ukraine's political processes could reduce the danger to "Russian speakers" or the new government gain legitimacy through elections. By describing the change of government as a "putsch" or "coup" the aim was to deny the agency of the protestors and drain legitimacy from Euromaidan. If this was how events were seen, as opposed to just propaganda, then it explains why Moscow misapprehended the state of public opinion in Ukraine, including in those regions with the warmest feelings toward Russia. Putin may also have an exaggerated view of the numbers of ethnic Russians in Eastern Ukraine.[2] One apparent concern was that a new Ukrainian government would revoke Russia's lease on the Sevastopol naval base, although it would have been in no position to do much about this.[3] Putin's first decisions, essentially reactive and with much still uncertain, determined the shape of the conflict that followed.

At this time Russian objectives could have been any of the following:

- To return Yanukovych to power.
- To gain leverage over events in Kiev, at best to revive the ECU project and at least to prevent a move toward the EU, and possibly NATO.[4]
- To cause sufficient chaos in Ukraine so that the government could not function and was unable to take any major initiatives.
- To cause the fragmentation of Ukraine so that Eastern Ukraine along with Crimea either split away from the West to form an independent country or joined Russia.
- To annex Crimea.

There are no indications that much effort was devoted to evaluating and weighing these objectives or working out what might have to be done to achieve them.[5] They may have coexisted in the minds of Putin and his advisors, with priorities shifting as circumstances changed. Snyder suggests that in the weeks prior to Yanukovych's flight papers were circulating in Moscow arguing that the Yanukovych regime was "utterly bankrupt" and that the aim must now be the "disintegration of the Ukrainian state," and that this would require a direct intervention rationalized on the basis that the West was stoking civil war, supporting fascists, and oppressing the Russian minority. The demand would be for Ukraine's "federalization," which would be tantamount to its dissolution.[6] This was a theme that was picked up in late February and through March. Much of this reflected an inability to take the idea of an independent Ukrainian state seriously and a tendency to assume that because its political institutions shared roots with those of Russia they were essentially the same had it not been for the corrupting influences of Western ideas. This distinctiveness of Ukraine's political culture and the resilience of its institutions, despite the corrosive effect of corruption, was underestimated.

Putin insisted that Yanukovych had been deposed illegally, but he saw him as a failure and never pushed hard for his return to power. His rhetoric at one level challenged no more than the legitimacy of Yanukovych's overthrow, pointing to a combination of Western interference and local neo-Nazis. At another level he challenged the territorial integrity of Ukraine, stressing the artificiality of its borders, with the implication that a sufficient shock could cause it to fragment. He referred to the region potentially in contention by its old but redundant name of Novorossiya, and noted that it was a relatively recent part of Ukraine. Such talk demonstrated that he at least thought a split in the country was a possibility, even leading to the Eastern part joining Russia. That would, however, confirm the loss of the rest of Ukraine to the EU and NATO. If he really wanted to maintain any leverage, then it was better that the East remain part of Ukraine. When, in March, Lavrov denounced the government in Kiev he combined this with demands for a federal structure.[7] Russia's key objective for Ukraine as a whole was to the shape its new political order in such a way that governmental decision-making would be paralyzed.

But this was combined with seizing Crimea. The attraction of this move to Putin was that it could be done straightaway and was not contingent upon how others responded. It was an exercise of control rather than coercion. It salvaged something from the wreckage of the previous Ukrainian strategy and might even trigger a more satisfactory chain of events. It was not a new idea.

The possibility that at some point Crimea might return to Russia had been around since the breakup of the Soviet Union and was revived whenever hostile forces seemed to be in power in Kiev. It had been discussed during the Euromaidan protests although little had been done by way of preparation. According to Putin he decided to act on February 23, as the old language law was being repealed in the Rada. This was the concluding day of the Sochi Winter Olympics. The Russians had poured resources and effort into this event, but it was now overshadowed by the drama close by. That day the Russian president told senior aides that events had "unfolded in such a manner that we had to start planning how to return Crimea to Russia. We could not leave the region and its people to the whim of fate and the nationalist steamroller."[8] There was little by way of preparatory staff work or consideration of the full implications of such a move.

Given the presence of a major base at Sevastopol, the home of Russia's Black Sea Fleet, taking Crimea was never going to be too challenging an operation. On February 26 a snap military exercise was ordered which provided cover for Russian paratroopers to be flown to Sevastopol airport. The main airports were seized and the Ukrainian navy was prevented from leaving port when four old Russian vessels were sunk at the mouth of the Donuzlav lagoon. On the morning of February 27 government institutions in Crimea were taken over by pro-Russian activists (the "Russian-speaking Crimean population's self-defense force"). This included the Parliament in the capital Simferopol. A new government was sworn in and a referendum on unity with Russia announced. A bill was introduced into the Duma to facilitate accession of new territories to the Russian Federation (removing a previous stipulation that required the agreement of the country from which

territory was seceding). On March 16, a hastily arranged referendum supported a re-integration of Crimea into the Russian
Federation. The official result from the Autonomous Republic of
Crimea was a 96.77 percent vote for integration of the region into
the Russian Federation with an 83.1 percent turnout.

The implausible numbers and the rushed process, with
elements of coercion, were easy to mock and underscored the
illegality of the annexation. Yet most observers believed that the
move had considerable local support.[9] If Putin had trusted his
claims about support in Crimea he might have agreed to a properly monitored referendum that would have produced a less overwhelming but more credible result and so given his move greater
legitimacy.[10] The group most opposed were the Tartars, who had
once been the majority group in Crimea and now constituted
some 13 percent of the population. They feared—correctly—that
they would suffer under a new regime.

Was the intention from the start to annex? Answering questions
on March 4 Putin said that it was not.

QUESTION: How do you see the future of Crimea? Do you consider the possibility of it joining Russia?
VLADIMIR PUTIN: No, we do not.

The rest of the answer, however, was carefully constructed:

Generally, I believe that only residents of a given country
who have the freedom of will and are in complete safety can
and should determine their future. If this right was granted
to the Albanians in Kosovo, if this was made possible in
many different parts of the world, then nobody has ruled

out the right of nations to self-determination, which, as far
as I know, is fixed by several UN documents. However, we
will in no way provoke any such decision and will not breed
such sentiments.[11]

The qualification was crucial, for he was saying that the people of
Crimea could themselves decide to join Russia as an act of self-
determination along Kosovo lines. All he was disclaiming was
Russian responsibility in prompting such a move.

The first proposal for a referendum on February 27 was for
one that would acknowledge Crimea as a "self-sufficient state"
but within Ukraine. From the perspective of the new pro-Russian
leadership in Crimea the risk of a middle course was of ending up
like an unrecognized statelet such as South Ossetia. Better to get
the full benefits and protection of Russian sovereignty. Moreover,
it was unclear how a middle way could work for Putin, with a position in Crimea that was illegal yet could not be relinquished.[12]
(These were two issues that later dogged the Russian position in
Donbas). At the same time he needed to be sure that his position could hold. Putin was watching to see if there was any move
from Kiev or elsewhere that could disrupt the transfer of sovereignty. According to one source, who was organizing volunteers
in Crimea at the time, it was not until March 6 that they were
allowed to talk about unification with Russia. This source
suggested that Moscow was waiting to see how Ukraine's military
would respond. When it became clear that they had no capacity
for a serious confrontation (although some Ukrainian military
bases did resist), the Russian agents were allowed to unfurl the
many Russian flags shipped in for this purpose.[13]

Crimea was annexed by Russia after the referendum. In his address on March 18, 2014, Putin repeated the allegations about the illegitimacy of the new Kiev government and contrasted this with the determination of the Russian-speaking majority in Crimea to protect themselves against the retrograde elements. He referred to the 1999 NATO campaign against Serbia and the eventual independence of Kosovo to demonstrate the West's double standards when it comes to international law. The main thrust of his analysis, however, was to emphasize how events in Kiev were part of a pattern. The "color revolutions" were "controlled." They did those who acted in their name little good for in practice they were "aimed against Ukraine and Russia and against Eurasian integration." Confirming that Russia acted out of a sense of threat he used a dramatic metaphor: "Russia found itself in a position it could not retreat from. If you compress the spring all the way to its limit, it will snap back hard."[14]

There were two features of the Crimean operation that foreshadowed the coming stages of the conflict. The first was the use of professional soldiers in uniforms without markings (the so-called "little green men"). Having first denied their direct involvement, including in private conversations with German chancellor Angela Merkel, Putin eventually admitted their role:

> our soldiers, of course, stood behind the self-defense forces of Crimea. They acted very civilly, and as I said, decisively and professionally. It otherwise wouldn't have been possible to hold an open, honest and dignified referendum and help people to express their opinion.[15]

Later he was even more explicit:

> I gave the orders and instructions to the Ministry of Defense,
> why hide it, under the guise of protection of our military
> facilities in Crimea, to deploy a special division of the Main
> Intelligence [Directorate] (the GRU) together with naval
> infantry forces and paratroopers.[16]

The second feature was flexibility when it came to local leadership. The first to be asked to lead Crimea into Russia was the existing Crimean prime minister, Anatoly Mogilev, but he refused. Next was an eccentric Communist Leonid Grach, who was tempted but was then passed over as it became apparent that he had no following. Sergey Aksyonov, the head of the Russian Unity Party, attracted attention during clashes between Tartars (hostile to a return to Russia) and pro-Russians in Simferopol. Although rumored to have criminal connections, he was soon sworn in as prime minister, endorsed by the self-exiled Yanukovych.

DONBAS

A detailed opinion poll conducted in the middle of March 2014 provides a valuable snapshot of Ukrainian opinion on the eve of the annexation of Crimea. This showed that Euromaidan had grown in support since the fall of Yanukovych's government and that there was continuing backing for an Association Agreement with the EU (although not membership in NATO). New presidential elections, already announced, were also welcomed as a means by which to legitimize the new political order. The polling also confirmed the image of a deeply divided country, with Western and Central Ukraine sympathetic to Euromaidan and its demands while Southern (still including Crimea and Sevastopol) and Eastern Ukraine were generally unsympathetic. Yet the picture was nuanced. One could infer from the results the extent of the support in Crimea for the move to join Russia. In Eastern Ukraine, however much the fondness for Russia and irritation with the recent turn of events, there was only limited concern about discrimination against ethnic Russians. There was no backing for active Russian intervention to support the rights of ethnic Russians (and even those who considered themselves ethnic Russians were evenly divided on the matter). By and large people wanted to keep the country as a unitary state rather than see it fragment or even become more federal (although that was a demand with some support in the East).[17]

Demonstrations and occasional occupation of government buildings by anti-Maidan forces appeared in Eastern Ukraine from early on. Putin appears to have hoped for a much more generalized pro-Russian insurrection. On March 1, Russia's upper house of parliament approved President Putin's request for Russian forces to be used in Ukraine "until the normalization of the political situation in the country."[18] Russia maintained a substantial military capability on its side of the border in a position to invade, underlined by warnings about a possible direct Russian military intervention in a "peace-keeping" role. Some forty thousand Russian forces were kept in position, on occasion engaging in exercises to demonstrate that they were ready to cross the border. Moscow therefore gave itself reasons and authority to invade. In addition efforts were made to undermine an already weak Ukrainian economy by export embargoes and threats to gas supplies. Putin's rhetoric gave every impression that a large swathe of Ukraine would be a natural fit for Russia and that it would be perfectly reasonable for this to be demanded by the people of the region.

Sergei Glazyev, a former Communist and presidential candidate, had been appointed by Putin in 2012 as an advisor, tasked with coordinating the work of federal agencies developing the Eurasian Customs Union. He was known for hard-line and nationalist positions. In 2013 he had been at the fore in warning Ukraine against opting for the EU (telling Kiev this would be "suicide"), and as Euromaidan gathered pace he had accused the US of arming rebels and supporting a coup.[19] His position was deeply opposed to "the Nazis" in Kiev. In an interview published in March 2014 he emphasized that the Crimeans had acted on their own volition in response to atrocious acts by Ukrainian nationalists and that now Eastern Ukraine was "inching closer to civil war." He envisaged a situation when "it will be not just Russia, but also the international community that would protect people." If this happened it "would be a direct consequence of the fact that, at present, neo-fascists in the South-East of Ukraine are committing outrages, resorting to armed violence, to lynch law, to the burning of houses of people they don't like."[20]

In 2016 the Ukraine prosecutor general's office published audio tapes of telephone conversations involving Glazyev, recorded over a number of days, staring on February 27, seeking to orchestrate civil unrest in Eastern Ukraine. A key passage comes from a conversation on March 1. This is as transcribed and published:

I have an order to raise everybody, to raise people. People should gather in the square to demand turn to Russia for help against "Banderovtsy" [alleged followers of Stepan

Bandera but effectively all supporters of Kiev]. Specially trained people should knock out "Banderovtsy" from the building council, and then they should arrange the meeting of the regional state administration, gather executive authorities. Collect regional executive committee and give him the executive power and subordinate police to this new executive. I have direct orders—to raise the people in Ukraine where we can. So we must take people to the streets, so do as in Kharkiv [where demonstrations had taken place] and as soon as possible. Because as you see the president has signed a decree, operation began, here has reported that the military are raised. What are they waiting for? We cannot do everything with force, we use the power to support people, not more. And if there are no people, what support there might be?

In another conversation with an activist in Odessa, Glazyev explains that "It is very important that people appeal to Putin. Mass appeals directly to him with a request to protect, an appeal to Russia, etc."[21]

The strategy was clear enough. As was notionally the case with Crimea, a popular movement must be generated that could then appeal to Russia for support. Activists were reported to be being bussed into cities across Eastern Ukraine. Russian TV networks hailed the protests. Russia's permanent mission to NATO posted on Twitter a map of Ukraine with superimposed images of Russian flags in 11 Ukrainian cities where protests had taken place, including Odessa, Dnipropetrovsk, Kharkiv, and Donetsk.[22] But the counter-Kiev demonstrations in Eastern Ukraine were not well supported and the early effort fizzled out.

If they had taken off then this might have led to a much more substantial intervention from early on, with which Ukraine would have struggled to cope.

The anti-Kiev effort was revived in April, and this time the rebels managed to establish a territorial base. In some places, for example Kharkiv, the initial moves to seize buildings were rebuffed and the would-be rebels arrested. On April 7 Russia complained about military force and the "Right Sector" militia being used to suppress dissidence. Acting Ukrainian president Turchynov warned that "a second wave of the Russian Federation's special operation against Ukraine [has] started" with the "goal of destabilizing the situation in the country, toppling Ukrainian authorities, disrupting the elections, and tearing our country apart."[23] A few days later, on April 12, masked men in army fatigues and bulletproof vests armed with Kalashnikov rifles captured a number of state buildings in Sloviansk.[24] This was followed by intensive fighting, which continued for some time (leading in late May to the loss of a Ukrainian helicopter carrying fourteen soldiers, including a general).

The group entering Sloviansk was led by an eccentric adventurer, inspired far more by imperial Russia than Bolshevism, called Igor Girkin, whose nom de guerre was Igor Strelkov (the "shooter"). He was believed to be a former member of the GRU and a participant in the 1992 operation to separate Transnistria from Moldova and the Serb war in Bosnia. In a November 2014 interview he claimed to have set in motion the "flywheel of war" and "reshuffled the cards."[25] He had commanded a militia unit in Crimea where he had been seen as an authoritative figure with good contacts in Moscow. With Crimea sorted he had become alarmed by the lack of activity elsewhere. "Crimea and Novorossiya together had been the jewels in the crown of the Russian Empire," but if they were kept separated that just left "Crimea on its own attached to a hostile state, severed from the mainland." With Kiev still in disarray anti-Maidan activists made their way to Crimea to discuss with him what they might do to start their own rebellion. On his account they were not being directed by Moscow but assumed that if their movement developed enough momentum then "Russia would lend a hand." It is probable that Putin's man, Glazyev, knew what was going on. He certainly became active in providing support. With 52 armed volunteers who had served with him in Crimea Strelkov made his way to Sloviansk, a city large enough to be notable but small enough for this group to be able to make a difference. In the first instance there were probably no more than six hundred fighters supporting the total separatist effort.[26]

It was not long after this that Putin started to talk openly of Novorossiya, suggesting that he saw genuine possibilities in the developing upheavals in Eastern Ukraine. Yet it soon became apparent that support for the breakaway movement was at best patchy. In Donetsk and Luhansk referendums were scheduled for May 11, 2014. Putin, perhaps aware that the separatists were overreaching, urged delay. They still went ahead with the expected results, which the Kremlin said it "respected." There was no response to the request from Donetsk that the new entity be "absorbed" into Russia.[27] Instead a Donetsk People's Republic was established with Alexander Borodia as prime minister and his friend Strelkov defense minister. A separate Luhansk People's Republic was also established. These were both only parts of their respective provinces. The two never fused into one entity for governance purposes. In addition their political purpose was unclear, reflecting the confusion in Russian objectives mentioned earlier. Those involved wanted to follow Crimea out of Ukraine and into Russia, but Moscow wanted them to remain part of Ukraine so that they could influence Ukrainian politics into the future. Strelkov later observed mournfully:

> We thought, the Russian administration will come, logistics will be organized by Russia and there would be another republic within Russia. And I didn't think about any kind of state building. And then, when I realized that Russia will not take us in; this decision was a shock for us.[28]

There was an evident tension between carving out a chunk of Ukraine that would be effectively controlled by Russia on the one hand and gaining influence over Ukrainian decisions to prevent moves inimical to Russian interests on the other. This tension was never resolved.

These entities were not self-sufficient. They depended on Russian support, and whatever explanations offered by the Kremlin, Russia in effect owned them. NATO Supreme Allied Commander General Philip Breedlove commented upon the military training and equipment of these pro-Russian "activists," including their weapon-handling discipline, coordinated use of tear gas and stun grenades against targeted buildings, speed in establishing roadblocks and barricades in the surrounding area, and professional manning of checkpoints.[29] In order to avoid the legal issues raised by dispatching troops into another's territory, the Russians claimed that these individuals had been doing no more than responding to surges of popular feeling among fellow Russians unfortunate enough to live outside Russia proper. But denying an active Russian role was never plausible.[30] The Kremlin had backed agitators in the hope that they would have a major political effect, without being sure what that effect would be. It was not even able to ensure that its agents would act in such a way as to maximize their effectiveness.

The Ukrainian government, still in a chaotic state, was unable to do much about these seizures. It avoided provocation, perhaps to avoid giving Russia the sort of pretext provided by the Georgians in 2008, although even if it had wanted to provoke at first it was in no position to do so. There was no capacity for any heroic battle.[31] Local figures in the security apparatus had little confidence in Kiev and were not going to resist a movement with which many had sympathy. At first there was some support for the agitation from local Ukrainian oligarchs, who recognized the degree of discontent with Kiev. But they had no interest in a secessionist movement. It would be bad for business. They were reluctant to get into competition with the much better organized Russian oligarchs.

The modest scale of pro-Russian demonstrations in Eastern Ukraine thus did not support claims that Russia must rescue people who faced danger and were desperate for assistance. It also warned Moscow of the problems that could arise should it attempt a full-scale occupation. There were other areas of agitation in addition to Donetsk and Luhansk but they gained little traction. Odessa was of obvious importance as a regional capital. On May 2 there was a tragic incident in the city. After violent clashes between pro-Russian demonstrators and pro-unity supporters, the separatists were overwhelmed and retreated to a trade union building, which caught fire after petrol bombs had been thrown back and forth from and into the building. Forty-two people died as a result. The incident aggravated already tense relations in southeastern Ukraine, and was seized upon by Moscow and its local agents to demonstrate the vicious nature of the anti-Russian movement, but it also ended the idea that Odessa was available as a separatist stronghold.

Even in Donetsk and Luhansk the Russian position was not as strong as it had been in Crimea. There was no evidence that those occupying buildings were actively backed by substantial sections of the local population. Pro-unity demonstrations drew signifi-cant crowds, but meager compared with those that had filled the streets of Kiev. The overall impression was of a population who would like more autonomy but had no interest in joining Russia. An opinion pollster reported:

> 18.1% of Donetsk and 24.2% of Luhansk support the recent armed seizures of administrative buildings in Donbas region, while surrounding provinces overwhelmingly disapprove of the current situation. 72% of Donetsk and 58.3% of Luhansk residents disapprove of the current actions. Roughly 25% in Donbas region said they would attend secessionist rallies in favor of joining Russia.

Support for closer ties with Russia was actually down from pre-crisis levels.[32] This lack of enthusiasm raised a problem for Moscow that limited its options. The forced annexation of a sizeable portion of Ukraine would have left Moscow facing the problems of administering an uncooperative population living in a territory of contested boundaries. Even in Crimea, where there had been popular support for annexation, there were soon reports of difficulties issuing passports, introducing the Russian currency, changing legal frameworks, keeping shops supplied, and a general collapse of the local economy.[33] The Russians had set in motion a chain of events that offered neither effective control of more territory nor effective coercion of the Ukrainian government and people.

INTERNATIONAL RESPONSES

In addition to the impact on Ukraine Putin's moves affected other countries in the former Soviet space. Demanding the right to veto unwanted developments in one sovereign country raised the possibility that the same right could be demanded elsewhere. Asserting a special responsibility to protect the position of Russians unfortunate enough to live outside the borders of the Russian Federation potentially affected a number of countries. This was already the rationale behind the frozen conflicts in Moldova and Georgia. It could be used to challenge the position of the Baltic States, notably Estonia,[34] and even Russia's notional partners in the Eurasian Union, Belarus and Kazakhstan. This was potentially a coercive threat, a warning to these countries not to meddle while Russia was sorting out its position with Ukraine. But it also created a general wariness of Russia that began to influence all of its foreign relations. If it was believed that Russia was capable of moving into a full expansionist mode, then Poland, Sweden, and Finland could come into the frame. "If I wanted," Putin is reported to have told Ukraine's president Poroshenko in mid-September, "in two days I could have Russian troops not only in Kiev, but also in Riga, Vilnius, Tallinn, Warsaw, and Bucharest."[35]

The West's response was generally cautious, too cautious for some. President Obama was accused of failing to appreciate the developing logic of President Putin's authoritarianism and his assertiveness both at home and in Russia's "near abroad."[36] Another allegation was that Putin's risk calculus had been eased because Obama had demonstrated his risk aversion when he hesitated on the verge of taking a forceful position after Syria's use of chemical weapons.[37] The Western response to the annexation of Crimea was derided as feeble. Former British foreign secretary Malcolm Rifkind commented:

> On the basis of the measures announced so far by both the US and the EU, on visa controls and asset freezes internationally, I say with great sadness that is a pathetic and feeble response that does not match the seriousness which those implementing these responses have themselves acknowledged we face at the present time.[38]

A reporter for the *Financial Times* observed that "In more than a dozen interviews, planners, security officials and members of the intelligence community have spoken of Moscow with universal, if grudging, praise". The Russian tactical campaign was described as being a "dexterous and comprehensive", "masterly", and campaign, and one step ahead at every turn.[39]

From the other direction the West was criticized for failing to pay adequate attention to the full implications of what was going on in Kiev in February 2014 and supporting what was, in the end, an anti-democratic seizure of power.[40] There was no evidence that Western public opinion was after a tougher stance,[41] or that there were many attractive options available if the aim was to force Moscow to reverse course.

The conflict over Ukraine represented a sharp geopolitical jolt, a reminder that hard power never quite goes away and that the role of force remained formidable when setting borders and changing regimes. The opening of the conflict was even accompanied by unnerving references to nuclear weapons. As Crimea was being annexed, the head of a Kremlin-backed news agency, Dmitry Kiselyov, observed on his TV program that "Russia is the only country that could really turn the US into radioactive ashes," against the backdrop of a mushroom cloud on a screen behind him.[42] In August 2014 Putin was reported as saying that other countries "should understand it's best not to mess with us," with a reminder that "Russia is one of the leading nuclear powers."[43] By the same token the crisis raised questions about the supposedly "soft power" of the EU and its role in reshaping the political and economic structures of post-Communist states. The EU had taken positions on an Association Agreement with Ukraine when it was well aware that this would require Kiev to meet tough conditions with major reforms taking many years. EU statements could often be misleadingly reassuring to its interlocutors yet alarming to those listening in.

A legacy of this tendency to offer calming undertakings to serve an immediate purpose, with little expectation of ever being called to account, was evident in the disregard of the security assurances contained in the December 1994 Budapest Memorandum. This marked Ukraine's agreement to relinquish almost two thousand nuclear weapons that had been left on Ukrainian territory following the breakup of the Soviet Union. The memorandum confirmed that these weapons would be dismantled and that Ukraine would ratify the Nuclear Non-Proliferation Treaty. In return it received a statement from Russia, the United States, and the United Kingdom, which was followed by France and China, extending security assurances to Ukraine. Ukraine's borders would be respected in line with the principles of the 1975 Final Act of the Conference and Security in Europe. There must be no use or threat of force against Ukraine, it should be supported if threatened by economic coercion, and any incident of aggression by a nuclear power should be brought before the UN Security Council. The situation in 2014 was hardly ambiguous. Ukraine was a victim of aggression and economic coercion. Despite what Kiev hoped and claimed, the language in the Memorandum fell short of "guarantees."[44] The Western powers could claim that they were responding as helpfully as they could to a difficult situation; for the Russians there was clearly no issue to be addressed.

The apparent irrelevance of the provisions of the Memorandum led to the observation that Ukraine would have been better off keeping its nuclear weapons. It would then have had its own deterrent and Russia would never have invaded. The problem with this counter-factual is that it would have been extremely difficult for Ukraine to hold on to its weapons. Its bargaining position in 1994 was not great. Even if Ukrainians had managed to replicate the launch codes, which they might have done given time, the warheads could only have been serviced in Russia. A determination by Ukraine that it wished to take the opportunity to become a full nuclear power would have created an immediate crisis with Russia, and also with the US, and would probably have been accompanied by a cutoff in gas supplies.[45] Nonetheless, this experience was unhelpful for the future management of nuclear proliferation. Weak security assurances offered in return for abandoning a nuclear option had no value.[46]

There was another agreement from the 1990s that was also ignored by Russia. The anomalous position of Crimea, and the base of the Russian Black Sea Fleet at Sevastopol, had notionally been resolved in 1997 with a Treaty of Friendship, Cooperation, and Partnership between Ukraine and the Russian Federation. The two countries agreed, under Article 2, to "respect each other's territorial integrity, and confirm the inviolability of the borders existing between them."[47] This was extended in 2010, guaranteeing Russia access to its Sevastopol base until 2042.[48] Again it was not unreasonable to take the view in Kiev that it had given Russia something that it badly wanted in return for a meaningless assurance.

The annexation of Crimea was taken to the UN. Moscow could exercise a veto as a Permanent Member of the Security Council, so the main value of the forum was a setting in which to demonstrate Russia's isolation. A draft Security Council resolution of March 15 reaffirmed Ukraine's "sovereignty, independence, unity and territorial integrity." It denied the validity of the referendum that Russia was organizing to legitimize Crimea's break with Ukraine. A nonbinding resolution was passed in the General Assembly. It dismissed the Crimean vote as "having no validity, (and) cannot form the basis for any alteration of the status of the Autonomous Republic of Crimea or of the City of Sevastopol." It was passed with one hundred votes in favor, eleven against, and fifty-eight abstentions.[49] When the referendum took place on March 16 it was challenged in terms of its conduct as well as in international law.[50] This meant that Crimea's entry into the Russian Federation was no more likely to be recognized by the wider international community than the quasi-independent

Abkhazia and South Ossetia, or even Lithuania, Latvia, and Estonia after they had been seized by the Soviet Union in 1940. Outside of the UN the United States and the European Union agreed on economic sanctions to punish Moscow for its assault on Ukraine's sovereignty. The sanctions signaled displeasure in a mildly punitive way, and were largely directed against individuals.[51] Those after July 2014 targeted key sectors of the Russian economy—arms manufacturers, banks, and state firms. By September the financial pressure on individuals and firms had been stepped up.[52]

Annexations challenge international norms, not even offering the fiction of being a temporary occupation by way of political cover. They are also hard to reverse. In 1990 Iraq had annexed Kuwait and, despite extensive economic sanctions, it took a major military operation undertaken by a coalition of great powers with backing from the Security Council for it to be liberated. Now Moscow could not abandon Crimea without an enormous loss of face. This introduced a problem into attempts to achieve a political settlement for which there was no obvious solution. Moscow's seizure of another state's territory could not be accepted. Nevertheless, a view quickly developed that it was unlikely that Russia could be coerced into handing Crimea back, and so the focus had to be on preventing Russia from taking more slices of the salami. The priority had to be to restore Ukrainian stability, helping it retain its remaining territorial sovereignty and support other vulnerable states.

When President Obama and Chancellor Merkel, the two key players on the Western side, met on May 14, they set out an agreed-upon view. They were determined 'to impose costs on Russia for its actions," "united in our support for Ukraine,

including the very important IMF program approved this week
to help Ukraine stabilize and reform its economy" and supported
the Ukrainian government's "right and responsibility to uphold
law and order within its territory." They urged a diplomatic solution but were clear that "if the Russian leadership does not change
course, it will face increasing costs as well as growing isolation—
diplomatic and economic." In the first instance their focus was
on deterring Russia from destabilizing the imminent Ukrainian
presidential election (which were scheduled for May 25). Merkel
said this was "crucial."[53] Any Russian-inspired disruption was
identified as a potential trigger for more severe sanctions, so arguably the fact that these elections were relatively undisturbed
could count as a success for deterrence.

Even when making threats the tone from Western capitals
was one of cautious reasonableness.[54] High-level conversations
continued with calls between national capitals, emergency ses-
sions of international organizations, and face-to-face meetings.
Western leaders tended to take a measured tone, watching
matters with "grave concern" and warning of unfortunate
consequences if Russia went too far. They did not stop having
regular conversations with President Putin.

Their main concern was to deter yet more Russian aggression.
Thus in announcing the limited sanctions, the EU observed:

> Any further steps by the Russian Federation to destabilize
> the situation in Ukraine would lead to additional and
> far-reaching consequences for relations in a broad range
> of economic areas between the European Union and
> its Member States, on the one hand, and the Russian
> Federation, on the other hand. The European Union calls

on Russia to return to developing a strategic partnership with the EU instead of isolating itself further diplomatically and economically.[55]

All cooperation with Russia was suspended, and moves were made to shore up confidence among Eastern European members, including preparations for sending more soldiers and equipment and more exercises. Air patrols were stepped up over the Baltic States and a US warship was sent to the Black Sea.[56] NATO members who might feel threatened by a more aggressive Russia, including those with Russian minorities, were reassured that the Article V obligations were firmly in place. Traditionally neutral countries such as Finland and Sweden began to reconsider their position vis-à-vis NATO.[57]

How far were Western countries prepared to go in support of Ukraine? President Obama made it clear that he saw no circumstances in which the United States would use armed force in connection with this crisis: "We are not going to be getting into a military excursion in Ukraine."[58] Merkel said Germany "will certainly not deliver weapons, as this would give the impression that this is a conflict that can be solved militarily."[59] This statement passed over the difference between a belief in military victory and recognizing that the ability to take and hold territory by military means might shape the outcome of eventual negotiations.

It was also clear that economic sanctions faced opposition, especially in those European countries that had substantial trading relationships with Russia.[60] Although Merkel took a robust position, many German political figures were reluctant to undermine the relationship with Russia that had been the basis for the Cold

War détente and had facilitated the country's unification. Other "realist" commentators, including Henry Kissinger, encouraged a cool geopolitical assessment and warned against taking positions that could not be backed in practice.[61]

On March 14, Secretary of State John Kerry met with Foreign Minister Sergei Lavrov in London, and then on March 29 in Paris, without Ukrainians present. Lavrov's proposals indicated that Russia's priority was to ensure that Ukraine respected its interests. The stress was on neutrality, federal structures, raising the status of the Russian language, continuing economic ties with Russia, and recognition of the result of the Crimean referendum.[62] The Ukrainians were present, as well as the EU, at further talks in Geneva on April 17, and these produced an outline agreement.[63] The agreement said nothing about the status of Crimea or the role of Russian troops. The constitutional proposals were stated in sufficiently vague terms for them to be acceptable to the Ukrainian government, who gained some de facto recognition from Russia by being accepted as interlocutors. The most important sentences referred to the need to dismantle the barricades and end the occupations in Donetsk and Luhansk, but there were no provisions for their implementation, other than that the situation be monitored by the Organization for Security and Cooperation in Europe (OSCE). This had once been favored by Moscow as a truly pan-European security institution but it was now giving little support to the Moscow line on events in Ukraine. While the agreement was generally disregarded, the inspectors did deploy and came to play an important role in providing objective and informed accounts of the situation on the ground.[64]

Where there was significant Western activity was with regard to the more substantial, but also more constructive, challenge of trying to revive and restructure the Ukrainian economy. Ukraine signed the political aspects of the Association Agreement with the EU. On March 5 it also agreed to a financial assistance package of at least €11 billion in loans and grants from the EU budget and EU-based international financial institutions.[65] More importantly the IMF was brought in to provide the funds without which the country would go bankrupt.[66] The conditions required by the Fund included measures to deal with corruption, manage debt, and introduce market reforms. The challenge of paying for Russian gas, the price of which was raised very steeply very quickly, added to the economic burdens. If the gas was turned off, that would be to the detriment of other European countries as well as Ukraine.

These initial responses to this developing tension contained the area of actual conflict. In the run-up to NATO'S Cardiff summit of early September 2014, which took place at the same time as the cease-fire negotiations in Minsk, President Obama's proposition that there could not be a "military solution" to the Ukraine crisis was adopted as something of a mantra.[67] The effect was to signal to both domestic audiences and Ukraine that NATO members were not going to get militarily involved. At most NATO countries were prepared to supply forms of military assistance to help the Ukrainians resist further Russian advances.

To encourage this reticence Russia worked to create a sense of menace in Europe: questioning the independence of the Baltic States, engaging in unauthorized overflights of NATO airspace, and sending a submarine into Swedish waters, and making nuclear threats against Denmark and the Baltic countries, and as well as military exercises. These may have encouraged NATO members to stay cautious, but as much as actual events in Ukraine

it also led them to take security issues more seriously and so reinforced NATO. More attention began to be paid by NATO to tan-
gible forms of reassurance to the Baltic States. NATO adopted a
"Readiness Action Plan" that established military bases in Eastern
Europe and a rapid response force to protect its members from
Russian incursions. It also committed financial and material support to Ukraine and regular military exercises on its territory. If
nothing else, NATO was provided with an answer to the question
of what it needed to worry about as it left Afghanistan.

For Russia the stakes had now moved well beyond the political
orientation of Ukraine. The thrust of post-1991 policy had been
to demonstrate that Russia was a modern and economically significant European power, entitled to its say in the affairs of the region. It now faced barriers and exclusions. The natural response
was to look East instead of West, and there was soon talk of
Russia reducing its dependence on Western markets by looking
to Asia. Sergey Karaganov, an influential figure in Russia's foreign
policy establishment, wrote that Western strategy misunderstood
the extent to which the struggle was about stopping "others
expanding their sphere of control into territories they believe are
vital to Russia's survival," and also the extent to which "Russia is
far stronger, and the west far weaker, than many imagine."[68]

UKRAINIAN COUNTER-OFFENSIVE TO FIRST
MINSK NEGOTIATIONS

Although there was evidence of intimidation by the separatists
and substantial support from Russia, the rebellion in Donbas
struggled because of a lack of popular backing. Referendums

held in support of separatism had little credibility and were not taken seriously internationally or even locally.[69] Gradually the role of Russian forces within Ukraine became more direct and overt, as the more irregular separatist forces were unable to cope. The conflict became less of an externally sponsored insurgency in Eastern Ukraine and more of a limited war between Ukraine and Russia.

Petro Poroshenko's election as president on May 25 demonstrated that at least for the moment Ukraine had held together and avoided the chaos Moscow had sought. The war had united Ukraine more than it drew it apart. Positive feelings among Ukrainians toward Russia declined from 88 percent in September 2013 to just 30 percent by May 2015, according to the International Institute of Sociology.[70] Even those in Eastern Ukraine, supposedly more sympathetic to Russia, came to view their neighbor less positively—down from 83 percent to 51 percent. Another poll showed a majority of Ukrainians outside the areas controlled by separatists supporting membership of the European Union, but only 13 percent wanting to join Russia's customs union. Another survey by the same institute showed that only 15.3 percent of Ukrainians would be willing to hand Donbas over to Russia in exchange for peace, and the number only rose to 26.4 percent when it came to meeting demands for substantial autonomy for Donetsk and Luhansk. There was general support for a peace process, although less so in the West. Most would not agree to renouncing integration with the EU for peace, although on membership of NATO the population was evenly divided.[71]

The Ukrainian military effort against the separatists, under the heading of an Anti-Terrorist Operation (ATO), had begun on April 11 as soon as the armed militants had appeared in

Eastern Ukraine. It was odd terminology, reflecting the tendency to cast all opponents as "terrorists" (the Russians had done the same thing) but it left the Russian role unspecified. It was limited in its effects although it was sufficient to prevent a takeover in Kharkiv. With only around six thousand truly combat-ready troops, early Ukraine efforts had to rely on the private militias of local oligarchs and volunteer battalions.[72] There was no real capacity to take back territory until activity was stepped up in May. Then the separatist forces struggled to cope. As a combination of local agitators, militants who had learned their trade in Chechnya and Georgia, and some Russian special forces and adventurers, they lacked coherence. Coordination was often poor and political leadership at times eccentric. Their methods alienated local people, and they used recklessly the sophisticated equipment with which they were provided. With Ukrainian forces becoming better organized, and prepared to deploy firepower more ruthlessly, they gave ground. A key moment came on May 26 when government forces used aircraft and helicopters to wrest control of Donetsk airport from the separatists, who took significant casualties. In early July Strelkov's group was forced out of Sloviansk (after using a psychiatric hospital as their final redoubt) and pulled back to Donetsk. Strelkov's presence had made Sloviansk the military command center, so this was considered an important victory for Kiev.[73]

According to Strelkov Kiev had become emboldened because of the lack of direct engagement by Moscow. It had refrained from sending in large-scale forces. This, he claimed, disappointed the separatists, who lacked the strength to cope with Ukrainian forces. "Initially I assumed that the Crimea scenario would be repeated: Russia would enter," he later reported. "That was the best scenario. And the population wanted that. Nobody intended to fight for the Luhansk and Donetsk republics. Initially everybody was for Russia." That was the purpose of the Donetsk and Luhansk referendums but instead Russia only responded with calls for "dialogue" with Kiev. Because their leaders had assumed they would be absorbed by Russia they had done little to create functional states.[74]

Russia saw that its clients were at risk.[75] It began to move more advanced equipment to the separatists, including anti-aircraft weapons as well as GRAD rockets. Surface-to-air missiles made the skies more dangerous for Ukrainian military aircraft, and a number were taken down. They also caused an international scandal when a Malaysian Airways flight was downed on July 17 by a missile fired from a Russian BUK system, causing the death of 281 passengers and crew. From the start the simplest and most credible explanation was that it had been shot down by separatists who assumed that the target was a Ukrainian transport. Social media comments from Strelkov, which were taken down after he realized what had happened, provide compelling evidence.[76] More evidence came in over time. Because Moscow could not admit that either its own forces or its proxies could be responsible for such a crime, it put forward a series of fanciful and contradictory alternative theories, from a shoot down by a Ukrainian fighter aircraft to a Ukrainian BUK to a bomb on board, none of which survived scrutiny. The consequence of its refusal to admit a mistake was to end up casting a solitary veto on a UN Security Council vote to prevent an international tribunal being set up to investigate the incident.[77] Western sanctions, first introduced after the annexation of Crimea, were intensified.

These events may have distracted the separatists' attention from the defense of their positions. As the controversy surrounding the loss of the airliner continued, Ukrainian forces slowly but surely pushed the rebels back to about half of their original holdings. The rebels held major cities like Donetsk and Luhansk as the Ukrainian army were in their outskirts. They fired at the Ukrainian positions and the Ukrainians fired back, often into populated areas with the inevitable civilian casualties. This may have hardened local opinion against the ATO, but the separatists' hold on territory was still being weakened. The prospect was that they would be first be pushed out of Donetsk and then Luhansk. On August 19 the government took the town of Ilovaisk from separatists.

This was the high point of the ATO. If the border crossings had been reached, the insurgency would have been defeated. Moscow decided to get a grip on the situation. It made a number of moves. One, though this may have added to rather than reduced Moscow's problems, was to give the separatist leadership more authenticity by replacing the Russian citizens who had initially taken charge with Ukrainians.[78] The militant groups in Donbas were becoming linked to criminal elements, often using their weapons to pursue their nonpolitical interests.[79] One notable departure was Strelkov—"too much of a loose cannon for the shadowy Moscow operatives running the war in Eastern Ukraine."[80]

Another move was to increase the supply of weapons. On August 14 the Ukrainians claimed to have destroyed a column of military vehicles as they passed through a separatist-controlled border crossing. The Russians then appear to have created a diversion with so-called humanitarian convoys, consisting of army trucks painted white, which were supposed to deliver assistance to the areas under siege. In many cases the vehicles were reported to be empty.[81] Ukraine objected as Russia refused to allow inspections of their contents. While this row got the attention, more deadly material, including Grad rocket launchers and self-propelled artillery, crossed the border in one of the many unguarded sections where there were no OSCE monitors. A mixed column of vehicles, included T-72 tanks, was spotted on August 26, followed the next day by another two columns entering Ukrainian territory from Russia. NATO officials, wary of escalating the situation, described this as an incursion rather than an invasion, but the intent was clear enough. Moscow continued to issue denials but the separatists were less concerned about pretending that they were not getting these reinforcements. In response Ukraine ordered national conscription.

A full-scale war between the two countries appeared much closer. At least one thousand Russian troops were said to be inside Ukraine, with another fifteen thousand on the border. The prime minister of the Donetsk People's Republic, Alexander Zakharchenko, reported before Russian troops engaged fully that twelve hundred fighters trained in Russia for four months, had crossed into Ukraine and were ready to fight, and were supported by 30 tanks and 120 armored vehicles. He later retracted. He told Russian media in late August that among the three thousand to four thousand Russian citizens fighting with the separatists were "many military men" on their "summer holidays."[82] When ten Russian paratroopers were captured the official Russian line was that they had crossed the border by accident (they were later returned home following an exchange for Ukrainian prisoners).

Eventually Russian officials spoke of "volunteers" joining the fight, especially after a number had been killed.

The battle for Ilovaisk resumed. Ukrainian troops were surrounded and on August 29 they surrendered. As many as three hundred soldiers were killed, including some who were attacked as they evacuated. Then Luhansk airport, which had been used as a base for Ukrainian forces shelling separatist positions, was destroyed. Ukrainian forces buckled under the new onslaught. As ground was lost in Donbas, the government had to suspend the antiterrorist operation to concentrate on defense. Potentially more seriously Russians seized the border town of Novoazovsk and threatened the port of Mariupol. This raised the possibility of a land corridor to Crimea, which with only sea links was proving a challenge for Moscow to keep adequately supplied. Ukrainian prime minister Arseniy Yatsenyuk told the New York Council on Foreign Relations that it was easy to deal with "Russian-led guerrillas and the Russian-led terrorists. But it's too difficult for us to fight against well-trained and well-equipped Russian military."[83]

Despite the growing ascendancy of Russian-backed forces, on September 5 an agreement on a cease-fire was reached at Minsk, signed by representatives of Russia, Ukraine, and the OSCE, as well as the leaders of the Donetsk and Luhansk People's Republics.[84] This was a significant but also surprising development. There was no mystery why Ukraine should welcome the opportunity to negotiate. It would struggle to cope with this more overt Russian pressure and needed a cease-fire to recuperate. Although public opinion was divided on how far to push the military campaign, Ukraine's combat losses had been heavy and the economy was in free fall. There was only limited capacity to escalate operations.[85] There had been clear signals from Western capitals that there would be no direct military assistance. The conflict was encouraging nationalist sentiment in Ukraine as well as Russia. Moscow's coercive diplomacy had been effective to the extent that Poroshenko accepted the need for compromise, in terms of more autonomy for the troubled regions and respect for Russian concerns.

Why then did Russia show an interest in a deal at this point when it appeared to be winning the war? It could have pressed on regardless. A deeper intervention carried risks, including a quagmire, getting bogged down in an occupation against a hostile population. It was one thing to shell Ukrainian positions and another to move in numbers against those positions. It was one thing to occupy territory with superior force, but another to administer and reconstruct the society and economy, as the United States and its allies had learned in Iraq and Afghanistan. In addition there were reports of significant casualties, causing consternation in Russia. The authorities went to great lengths to deny that the deaths had occurred in Ukraine. Those that could not be denied relied on the fiction that individuals had temporarily left the army and volunteered to help the separatists.[86] Another reason for the deal was to establish a route for lifting Western economic sanctions as well as not providing an excuse for more. Under other circumstances Russia might have disregarded them, but the economy was slowing down prior to the crisis and then had to cope with a significant decline in the price of oil. From a high point of $115.9 per barrel Brent (the major trading classification for crude oil) on June 19, 2014, the price fell by 52 percent to $55.27 per barrel Brent by the end of the year.

The sanctions therefore were aggravating an already difficult situation. Some Russian responses, notably banning selected agricultural products from the EU, added to the costs and reduced the choices for Russian consumers. The prospect was one of squeezed living standards as the country faced a declining currency, recession, and high inflation, especially on foodstuffs.[87] In addition, although Russia met about a quarter of Europe's demand for gas,[88] the pressure on revenues limited the ability to threaten to cut supplies. In the past Russia had seen its energy exports as a potential source of political leverage; now it needed to confirm its reliability as a supplier. Putin told a Serbian interviewer on October 15, 2014, "I would like to stress that Russia is meeting its obligations in full with regard to gas supplies to European consumers. We intend to further deepen our cooperation with the EU in the energy sector, where we are natural partners, on a transparent and predictable basis."[89]

The sanctions were now increasingly geared to Russia's support of the separatists, especially after the shooting down of MH17. They affected investment in future exploration for the oil and gas industry. Western governments were explicit in linking easing of sanctions, or alternatively their potential intensification, with the implementation of the Minsk agreement. According to US deputy national security adviser Tony Blinken there was a need to make sure that "Russian personnel and equipment leave Ukraine, that the border is appropriately back under the control of Ukrainian forces and the Ukraine government, that it's monitored appropriately, and that there are buffer zones on both sides."[90]

Although there were good reasons for Russia to limit its ambitions in Ukraine, the position reached in early September was not naturally stable. Having separatists occupy a chunk of territory undoubtedly created a serious problem for Ukraine, but the amount held was not enough to advance Russia's original objectives. At about 7 percent of Ukraine's total it was too small to make much sense as a stand-alone entity, incoherent both economically and politically. At the same time it was also large enough (about the size of Belgium) to require a substantial subsidy to avoid internal disarray. Industrial production had collapsed and provisions had to be found to sustain people through the winter. In this respect, the new territories controlled by Russia joined those that had been seized from Moldova and Georgia as economic failures. Because Mariupol had not been taken there was still no obvious way to ease Crimea's problems, aggravated by the lack of a direct land route from Russia.[91]

One approach might have been to cash in the gains, as had been done with Crimea in March, and annex the enclaves in Donetsk and Luhansk. But this would result in continuing tension with Ukraine and preclude any sort of negotiated settlement. It would also mean continuing indefinitely with high levels of military mobilization and economic separation from the West, policing a 400-kilometer (250-mile) border. Meanwhile Ukraine would be bound to work even more closely with Western Europe.

Russia had regained the upper hand in the fighting but its underlying position was not that strong. This helps explain why the principles incorporated by the Minsk agreement seemed to suit Kiev as much as Moscow. The agreement was largely based on a plan originally proposed by Poroshenko in June. It dealt with disaffection in Eastern Ukraine by offering a degree of decentralization of power, protection of the Russian language, political and economic reconstruction in the enclaves, liberation of hostages and amnesties, withdrawal of illegal armed formations,

and a buffer zone on the border; OSCE was assigned a substantial role in monitoring implementation. A further agreement of
September 19 required that heavy weaponry be pulled back 15
kilometers (9.3 miles) from the line of contact, banned offensive operations and flights by combat aircraft over the security
zone, and withdrawal of foreign mercenaries.[92] On September
24 NATO reported a "significant," although not complete, withdrawal of Russian troops from Ukraine.[93] As the amount of support from regular Russian forces fell back the separatists made
little further military progress. Against Mariupol they appeared
to give up quite quickly, other than for occasional shelling, because of the entrenched position of Ukrainian forces.

The implementation of the political aspects of the agreement required the cooperation of the separatist leaders. Russia
did not endorse full independence for the enclaves, let alone annexation. It accepted that they would stay part of Ukraine but
with a significant amount of autonomy in return. The obvious
questions were how much autonomy, and would regional representatives be in a position to block the eventual accession of
Ukraine to the EU or vote for combination with Russia? If the
political representatives of the region were chosen by truly free
elections the separatists were unlikely to win. Elections they
conducted on their own rules would not be taken seriously. There
was certainly no reason to expect any substantial pro-Russian
sentiment in the Kiev parliament. In the October 26 Ukrainian
elections the Party of Regions, in the past sympathetic to Russian
interests, did not stand. In addition, the elections could not take
place in the territory held by separatists.

The separatists showed no interest in Minsk. Igor Plotnitsky,
head of the Luhansk People's Republic, observed that "sooner or

later, we will become part of the Russian Federation."[94] His fellow signatory to the Minsk agreement, Zakharchenko of the Donetsk People's Republic, claimed that he was forced to sign, and that this was an act of "betrayal." One of his deputies rejected the agreement to return control of the border to Ukraine.[95] Zakharchenko observed on October 18 that "We can no longer live in one state with Ukraine. Most likely, we will stay unrecognized. On the one hand, this seems bad. On the other hand, it is very good for the economy. Being unrecognized means more money. This means no international obligations."[96] Two days later he declared the cease-fire over.

Putin faced the dilemma of being accused of betrayal if Donetsk and Luhansk were re-integrated into Ukraine or else accepting a loss of influence over Ukraine, and an intensified international crisis, if they effectively became part of Russia. Putin dare not abandon the separatists yet he was also unable to get them to meet their obligations. His unwillingness to force them to do so was one reason for the lack of progress at a meeting in Rome on October 17 involving Putin, Poroshenko, and EU leaders.[97] The lack of progress on the political side limited Moscow's ability to restrain Kiev's policy in relation to the EU. Following Minsk, Russia continued to demand that Ukraine not get closer to the EU. During a trilateral EU-Russian-Ukrainian meeting on September 12, 2014, it was agreed to postpone the implementation of the EU's Deep and Comprehensive Free Trade Agreement with Ukraine, from November 2014 to the end of 2015.[98] Russia threatened tariffs for Ukrainian exports to Russia should implementation take place. The conciliatory stance adopted by Kiev led to the resignation of the ukrainian deputy foreign minister. Nonetheless the line from Brussels was that "The European

Union will not allow Russia to dictate conditions for the EU's relations with Ukraine." The trilateral agreement did not prevent
ratification of the treaty by both the Ukrainian and European
parliaments. President Putin wrote to European Commission
president José Manuel Barroso, demanding that it be changed
before implementation and threatened "immediate and appropriate retaliatory measures" against Kiev if implementation went
ahead.[99]

So while significant levels of fighting and associated economic
costs were sufficient to create interest in a cease-fire they had not
created the conditions necessary for a long-term settlement acceptable to the key players. Without a settlement, a cease-fire became hard to sustain. It was preferable to live with the conflict
rather than make irrevocable compromises. Ukraine, supported
by Western countries, demanded the return of occupied territory.
Russia demanded that Ukraine come to terms with the new reality by accepting the annexation of Crimea and negotiating directly with separatist groups on a new constitutional settlement.
The situation remained unstable. Russia had damaged but not
defeated Ukraine. By sticking to economic sanctions, NATO and
the EU had damaged but not defeated Russia.

STALEMATE

The violence within Ukraine was continuing and unsettling. The
costs were high. By October 8, 2014, the conflict had claimed
3,682 lives and 8,871 wounded in Eastern Ukraine.[100]

As the first Minsk initiative petered out, there were once again
reports from NATO sources that Russian tanks, artillery, and

troops had entered Ukraine. Soon the focus was on Donetsk airport, which had come to symbolize Ukrainian resistance to Russian pressure. It had first been captured by the separatists and then recaptured in May by Ukrainian forces. This was seen at the time as a demoralizing blow to the separatists. Thereafter efforts to regain the airport had been regularly rebuffed by Ukrainian defenders, although at the price of wrecked buildings. This separatist failure left many casualties and undermined claims to be controlling the region. In addition, the separatists launched an offensive against the town of Debaltseve, which had been retaken by Ukrainian forces the previous July and was important in maintaining communications between Luhansk and Donetsk.

According to NATO's secretary-general, Russian troops were "supporting these offensive operations with command and control systems, air defense systems with advanced surface-to-air missiles, unmanned aerial systems, advanced multiple rocket launcher systems, and electronic warfare systems."[101] Yet most reports from the separatist areas were of local forces that were poorly organized and motivated. They had limited success for the energy expended. Ukrainian units held out in the Donetsk airport for a number of months. But eventually, the separatists' superior firepower got results. In January 2015, the airport fell.[102]

The battle for Debaltseve was even more ferocious. As it was a wedge, with separatist forces on both sides, the large Ukrainian garrison was cut off and denied supplies. As with the earlier and costly battle of Ilovaisk the government was accused of putting large numbers of troops into a vulnerable position without adequate support, leading to a drawn-out and painful retreat and hundreds of both military and civilian casualties.[103] A number of other towns and villages were seized, although the presumed next major target, the coastal city of Mariupol, stayed with Ukraine despite being subjected to regular shelling.

Against this background, in February there were once again talks in Minsk, this time filling in some of the details from the agreement of the previous September. As a cease-fire, this was no more effective than that agreed to the previous September. The Package of Measures called for:

- an immediate and comprehensive cease fire
- withdrawal of all heavy weapons from the contact line by both sides
- commencement of a dialogue on modalities of local elections
- legislation establishing pardon and amnesty in connection with events in certain areas of Donetsk and Luhansk regions
- release and exchange of all hostages and unlawfully detained persons
- safe access, delivery, storage, and distribution of humanitarian assistance on the basis of an international mechanism
- defining of modalities for full resumption of socioeconomic ties
- reinstatement of full control of the state border by the government of Ukraine throughout the conflict area
- withdrawal of all foreign armed groups, military equipment, and mercenaries from Ukraine
- constitutional reforms providing for decentralization as a key element and local elections in certain areas of Donetsk and Luhansk regions[104]

One issue was whether these were measures that should be followed in a logical order, completed by the elections, or else, as the Russians argued, a process in which different elements could be pursued in parallel. The Ukrainians argued that no free elections could take place until the territories had been reintegrated and "all foreign armed groups, military equipment, and mercenaries" had been withdrawn. As before, the separatist leaders Zakharchenko and Plotnitsky signed up but without enthusiasm. "Will we be part of Ukraine?" Plotnitsky asked. "This depends on what kind of Ukraine it will be. If it remains like it is now, we will never be together."[105]

From the start, this was more a "less-fire" than a cease-fire. The fight for Debaltseve continued even after the cease-fire had supposedly come into effect, but once that was taken there were no major military breakthroughs. Through April and May, there were regular reports of a major build-up and movements of Russian men and equipment within the separatist-held areas. NATO commander General Breedlove warned at the end of April that Russia was taking advantage of the nominal cease-fire to reposition its troops and equipment and to train and supply the separatists who were preparing for a new offensive.[106] There were also suggestions that Russia had sought to get the separatist command and control in better working order. In May Poroshenko claimed:

the total number of the enemy force in Donbas taking into account members of illegal armed groups is more than 40,000 people, while the Russian military grouping near the state border totals over 50,000 servicemen, almost 1.5 times more than in July 2014.[107]

A consensus was reported to be building "among NATO officials and military analysts of the situation in Eastern Ukraine that Russia will renew its invasion of the region in the next two months."[108] In late June 2015 the United Nations reported that 6,500 people had perished in the past year of the conflict, along with 16,000 wounded and 5 million in need of aid.[109]

At the start of June, a separatist offensive was launched against the town of Maryinka, some eighteen miles away from Donetsk.[110] The assault was beaten back by Ukrainian forces, with the separatists taking the heavier casualties. This was an important moment, especially after some unimpressive performances by the Ukrainian military. At Maryinka they displayed a much higher level of professionalism, using available forces and reserves with more agility. If this level of professionalism could be sustained and developed, Moscow could not rely on walkovers if it sought to take more territory. The importance of this moment may have been masked by anxieties about Russia's next steps. Ukraine moved men and equipment to what now seemed to be a vulnerable point: an area well on the Ukrainian side of the cease-fire line. The next day, Poroshenko warned of the prospect of a "full-scale" Russian invasion.[111] This was followed by more shelling and smaller operations around Donetsk. Yet for all the warnings of a new Russian offensive none materialized.[112]

In line with the Minsk agreements, and brokered by the OSCE, Ukrainian troops were withdrawn from the town of Shyrokyne, located just east of Mariupol, and plans announced for further demilitarization for Mariupol itself, with heavy equipment being moved and only infantry and small arms remaining. This would meet the Minsk requirement for a 30-kilometer (18.6-mile) buffer zone, free of heavy weaponry, along the front line. This followed a separatist withdrawal from the town a few weeks earlier. A month later, separatists pulled out of the town, describing this as "an act of good will and the demonstration of peaceful intentions."[113]

By keeping Ukrainian forces on the defensive and preparing for a possible invasion it kept them from mounting their own offensives against separatist positions. Ukrainians could not be sure about the targets of separatist attacks, and exposed units could be caught out. Those in fixed positions were vulnerable to shelling. There were therefore regular casualties. The possibility of a more substantial operation, even if short of a full invasion, might embarrass Ukrainian forces, as they had been embarrassed by the failure in Debaltseve, and so weaken Ukrainian resolve. To this was added a developing campaign of terrorism and subversion within Ukraine in order to further unsettle the country.[114] The challenge for Moscow was to sustain this pressure. Maintaining some fifty thousand troops close to Ukraine, and having some operating within, was expensive and wearing on the troops.

Moscow's pretense that it was not directly engaged in fighting in Ukraine caused it a problem. The charade was exposed regularly, yet the Russian authorities stuck to the same line. Arguably as the claim of "no-involvement" never had credibility, there was not much extra credibility to be lost with an even more substantial intervention, but an offensive that went well beyond anything the separatists could manage by themselves would make it impossible to maintain the fiction of noninvolvement. This is what had happened in August 2014. There was already sensitivity in Russia over the question of casualties. Deaths were covered up and troops disavowed if captured in Ukraine.[115] Documenting losses was the most newsworthy aspect of the report completed after the assassination of opposition leader Boris Nemtsov in February 2015. This referred to the deaths of 220 soldiers, while suggesting that the actual number was higher.[116] This issue became so sensitive that disclosure of combat deaths as a result of "special operations" in peacetime was prohibited.[117] There were also reports of desertion.[118]

Neither side had a strategy for bringing the conflict to a conclusion. The arguments against an offensive remained as powerful as they had been in 2014. The Russians could expect tough resistance from the Ukrainians, whose armed forces were steadily improving as they learned from experience and benefitted from Western-supported efforts at reform and improved training.[119] The greater the improvement, the greater the mainstream military commitment required from Russia to gain ground in an invasion. Russian strategy moved to one of securing the longer-term position of Luhansk and Donetsk by training and equipping local forces and putting them under Russian command. The local politics remained complicated. There was still no agreed government for the two "People's Republics," which maintained distinct structures.

The Context Shifts

From late 2015 the broader international context of the conflict changed. The first factor was the growing Russian role in the Syrian conflict that revived its position as a consequential power. The second was evidence of attempts to disrupt Western societies by subversive means, including cyber and information operations. Unlike military force or economic sanctions, which had a coercive value because these could be turned on and off, these operations were covert and undertaken by individuals who did not show their hand. In the end their strategic value depended on creating sufficient internal pressures to lead to a change in policy or even government although even then the full consequences of these actions could not be foreseen.

SYRIA

When a civil war began in Syria in 2011 Moscow viewed it with misgivings, fearing a repetition of events in Libya. This time the potential victim was its only client in the region.[1] At first Russia dealt with the threat to President Bashar Assad by providing military assistance and diplomatic support, mainly by using its Security Council veto.[2] As with Western countries, Russia also worried about radical Islamist forces taking over the country. This worry was magnified by the number of Russian Islamists who had joined ISIS. This shared antiterrorist interest with the West was highlighted in the initial rationales for the major Russian intervention that began in September 2015.[3] Syria therefore provided an opportunity to boost Russia's international standing, either as a leader in the anti-ISIS coalition or as Assad's protector. This would get the US government to take it seriously as a global actor, and perhaps encourage it to ease off on the sanctions triggered by the intervention in Ukraine.

The intervention was prompted by the evident weakness of forces loyal to the regime, controlling barely 10 percent of Syrian territory, demoralized and poorly led, despite being reinforced by Iranian units and Shia militias. They faced a coalition of antiregime groups, including the al-Qaida affiliate Jabhat al-Nusra. In the summer of 2015, Moscow concluded that it could support Assad with air power. Later, Russia embedded advisors with regime forces as it realized just how weak and inept they were, but it drew the line at committing their own forces in any numbers to ground operations.

The risks to engagement in the toxic politics of the Middle East were highlighted soon after the intervention began in September 2015. In November, a Russian passenger plane from Cairo crashed with the loss of 224 lives, probably from a bomb on board.[4] In the same month a Turkish F-16 shot down a Russian SU-24M2 because it had strayed into Turkish airspace.[5] This followed Russian attacks on Turkmen militias in Syria as part of an effort to persuade Turkey not to get in the way of its operations. This created a risk of a direct encounter between a NATO member and Russia. Moscow's response was uncompromising; Putin called the incident "a stab in the back." There were soon warnings about economic consequences—the potential cancellation of a pipeline project, trade bans, labor contracts for Turks in Russia curtailed, chartered flights and holiday packages closed down.[6] As there was little Turkey could do on its own to make a difference to the wider situation in Syria, Ankara decided to cut its losses, apologize to Moscow, and restore normal relations. Eventually in June 2016, the Turkish president Recep Erdogan wrote to Putin expressing sympathy and "deep condolences" to the family of the victims.[7] Russia could see this as an example of successful coercion.

Although Moscow presented its intervention as an antiterrorist operation, it soon became clear that almost any group fighting the regime would be considered "terrorists." Putin's line, as explained at the UN, was that it was an "enormous mistake to refuse to co-operate with the Syrian government and its armed forces, who are valiantly fighting terrorism face-to-face." The Russian intervention required its aircraft to fly regular sorties, and that created risks of an unwanted clash with other air forces operating in the area, including those of the US forces engaged in anti-ISIS operations. This required "deconfliction" arrangements to which Washington, despite its reluctance to talk about anything substantive with Moscow, agreed. The need to avoid incidents also led to arrangements with Iraq, Iran, and Israel. As a result, the Americans ended up concentrating on working against ISIS with government forces in Iraq and the Kurds in Syria, leaving the anti-Assad forces alone to face Russian strikes.

By the spring of 2016 the momentum had shifted and the pro-Assad forces were on the ascendant. Regime change was now unlikely. Still, progress was uneven. Because Russia did not use its own force to hold territory, even when ISIS or other rebel groups had been pushed out, they could get an opportunity to return (as in the ancient city of Palmyra, which was liberated with great fanfare before being reoccupied by ISIS). The Russians made no more effort than had the regime in sparing civilians living in rebel-controlled areas. This became clear in late 2016 with the assault on the rebel-held city of Aleppo, which was battered into submission. This was later followed by allegations that Syria had used chemical weapons to clear out resistant areas. Russia deflected these allegations, using its position on the Security Council and claims that the evidence had been faked.

In contrast to Ukraine, Russia could claim that its support in Syria for the established government meant that it was in line with international law. In contrast to Ukraine as well, this move appeared to be successful. A client was kept in power along with access to a naval base. Russia became a major player in the Middle East, so the US had to work with Putin on Syrian and anti-ISIS issues. Those countries that had been backing rebel groups became less willing to use up resources and political capital to do so, and started to put more stress on cease-fires and humanitarian relief. When the Saudi king visited Moscow in October 2017, this arguably represented a major shift in the perception of Russia's role. In addition, the Russian military was able to use Syria to introduce new weaponry and refine their tactics.

Yet Russia was also now "trapped."[8] On occasion, it announced that its engagement was being cut back or even withdrawn. But Assad's regime was not strong enough to survive without continuing Russian support, and the situation was too unstable to attract international donors into the reconstruction effort. The fighting continued, and at the end of 2017 Russia suffered embarrassing losses: an air base was attacked by a rebel militia with the loss of seven aircraft, and another aircraft was shot down. Extraction required a political settlement but there was no basis for any sort of power-sharing agreement involving Assad. When Russia took the lead in an attempt to broker a peace in late January 2018 at a "Syrian congress of national dialogue" at Sochi, the effort foundered when it was boycotted by leaders of the opposition.[9]

Another problem was that separate conflicts had sprung up in Syria. To the north, the US was still conducting its anti-ISIS operations. In this they had been supported by the Kurds, but the Kurds were under pressure from the Turks who were worried about support for their own Kurdish community. To the south, Israel was getting anxious about the Iranians establishing a permanent base close to its border, and in February 2018 it attacked Iranian targets and Syrian air defenses after an Iranian drone was sent into Israel. In May Israeli strikes removed much of the Iranian infrastructure in Syria. Before these strikes Israeli prime minister Benjamin Netanyahu had visited Moscow. It appeared that Russia was content for Iran to be pushed back. It was better that Assad was a Russian puppet than a Syrian puppet. But this demonstrated the extent to which Russia, a major player in Syrian affairs, was getting caught up in geopolitical issues quite separate from its own core objectives.[10]

An incident which occurred in February 2018 showed some links between the methods used in the Ukrainian and Syrian conflicts. It illustrated the consequences of outsourcing to private operators to undertake activities that served state interests but with which the state might not wish to be associated. In 2011 Putin described private military contractors as "a way of implementing national interests without the direct involvement of the state." One figure who led the way in developing this capability was Lt. Col. Dmitri Utkin. He had a Special Forces background and after fighting in Donbas had set up "Wagner," a mercenary group recalling Utkin's military call sign. Wagner began in 2015 to get involved in Syria with as many as two thousand fighters and regular combat engagements. In 2016 they were largely withdrawn but some returned. They now worked for an oil and gas company operating in Syria, linked to Evgeny Prigozhin, whose background was in catering but had become a close and wealthy Putin ally. Wagner had a "hybrid" quality, engaged in business but also available to the state when and if needed.[11]

In February 2018, Russian fighters working for Wagner combined with a pro-regime Syrian militia in an offensive apparently geared to gaining control of Conoco oil fields near Deir ez-Zor. This area had been held by ISIS but was now held by the US-backed Syrian Defense Forces (SDF), which had a significant Kurdish component. As the pro-regime force shelled the SDF base, US commanders tried to warn their Russian counterparts of the risks being run but failed to get a response. The Americans responded with heavy air strikes and artillery fire, devastating the attacking force, including the Wagner contingent, leaving "several dozen" dead. The official line was that these were private citizens, acting for their own reasons and not for the Russian state.

The Russian military command in Syria viewed the incident as "dangerous amateurism."[12]

The main impact of Syria on Ukraine was to serve as a distraction. Russia escalated its engagement in Syria as it became apparent that the conflict with Ukraine had reached an impasse. Thereafter it took effort and resources away from Donbas and reduced further any interest in escalating the struggle against Kiev. Although Russia's relevance to any Syrian diplomacy meant that the US and other Western countries had no choice but to engage Putin more actively than before, this did not seem to have any discernible impact on the diplomacy surrounding Ukraine.

CYBER AND INFORMATION OPERATIONS

One of the features of Russian strategy was the growing prominence of cyberattacks and information campaigns. While both are consequences of the opportunities of the digital age, they are distinctive in their technical and organizational demands as well as their effects. Denial of service attacks had become quite regular features of Russian coercive practice, for example with Estonia in 2007 and Georgia in 2008. It was therefore unsurprising that there were cyberattacks on Ukraine soon after Euromaidan.[13] An investigation of a cut to the Ukrainian power supply in December 2015 noted the sophistication of the attack and that it had been under development for some time, with reconnaissance undertaken to study the networks to be attacked and then synchronized assaults prepared. The Ukrainian operators were helpless as the system was taken out of their control and orders sent to close substations. One of the curiosities of the attack was that despite its careful preparation, it only lasted six hours. One of the reasons for the timing might have been a recent hack by activists against substations supplying power to Crimea, leaving residents there without power. In this respect it served as a warning of how Russia might retaliate should there be any further attempts to cut off supplies to Crimea. The preparation, however, preceded this particular trigger.[14]

In October 2017, Russia was responsible for the Petya ransomware attack, involving a malicious data encryption tool being inserted into a legitimate piece of software. When a machine was infected, a ransom note appeared demanding payment in bitcoins. This was described by the British government as originally directed against "Ukraine's financial, energy, and government institutions, but its indiscriminate design caused it to spread farther, affecting other European and Russian businesses. The cost to individual companies was considerable."[15]

The hacking was not confined to Ukraine. Its variety and ubiquity can be illustrated by events only reported in 2018. In Germany, for example, the government reported that the federal system had been penetrated by Russian hackers, while in June energy providers claimed that efforts had been made to hack into their networks. Energy networks appear as the natural starting point for attacks designed to damage other countries (an attempt was made to attack US energy providers in March 2016).[16] While these attacks were not prompted by financial gain,[17] others clearly were. Russians became key figures in major frauds, with money stolen from banks and accounts stolen from web-based firms. In February 2018, a former senior figure in the US Justice Department described Russia as "increasingly responsible both for indiscriminate destructive cyberattacks

and for harboring cybercriminals who harm the global online economy."[18] That April, in a rare joint statement, the FBI,
the Department of Homeland Security, and the UK's National
Cyber Security Centre (NCSC) warned of a series of attacks that
had targeted routers and the protective hardware around them,
enabling spying, thefts of intellectual property, and "future offensive operations." The purpose of the alert was to encourage
companies and individuals to make themselves harder to hack.[19]
As with so much hostile Russian activity, because these attacks
were not admitted, any motives had to be inferred. They could
not be examples of coercive diplomacy because there was no obvious link to any bargaining process.

Despite the damage done by these attacks, most attention was
given to the use of social media to spread "fake news," either to
support military operations or else, and increasingly, to support
political operations against countries or individuals deemed un-
friendly. The information operations followed by Russia from the
start of the Ukraine conflict represented audacious and blatant
attempts to reshape Western politics to encourage a more sympathetic approach to its interests. Yet, although this may appear as a
Russian innovation, it must be kept in mind that from Moscow's
perspective the West had been using its propaganda outlets and
means of subversion brilliantly from the Cold War period and on
to the color revolutions. Now, by insisting that these movements
were the creations of malign Western influences, they could be
delegitimized and their authenticity denied. At the same time
the experience may have reinforced Moscow in its belief (going
back to Soviet days) that skillful propaganda could create such
movements. This encouraged the idea that public opinion could

be moved using compelling but manufactured evidence, inserted into popular discourse by means of social media.

The advantage of information operations was that they were relatively cheap and could cause significant disruption. In practice, much of the Russian effort was defensive, reinforcing efforts to deny anything that might appear illegal or otherwise reprehensible, insisting that its personnel were not directly engaged in Donbas nor had any responsibility for shooting down the MH-17 airliner, or were only attacking legitimate military targets in Syria. But there was also an offensive aspect, seeking to undermine Western governments and expose their vulnerabilities or else reinforce governments that were already sympathetic. This went hand in hand with more traditional forms of subversion. France's National Front reportedly received €9.4 million ($9.4 million) of financial support. Russia had long backed the right-wing Jobbik Party in Hungary.[20] During the height of the furor over the impact of large numbers of immigrants entering Germany in January 2016, the Russian-speaking community was used to spread rumors about "Lisa," a thirteen-year-old girl from this community allegedly gang-raped by migrants. The story was picked up by the German media until a police investigation discovered that the girl had run away from home to be with her boyfriend, who happened to be of Turkish origin. This inaccurate story was widely publicized through Russian propaganda outlets—such as *Russia Today (RT)* and *Sputnik*—and then though social media. Demonstrations were organized through Facebook, and Foreign Minister Sergei Lavrov suggested that the German police were unable to address such cases properly.[21] This episode had the effect of alerting German opinion to the risks of Russian disinformation and aggravating relations between the two countries.

Russian propaganda campaigns often backfired, with the result that international opinion of Russia reached a low point.[22] Some were quickly exposed, for example a cyber-attack on the opening ceremony of the 2017 Seoul Winter Olympics, with disruptions to the Internet, broadcast systems, and the Olympics website. By using North Korean IP addresses, this was done in such a way that North Korea might get the blame. This was at a time when South and North Korea were engaging in talks to reduce the tensions between the two. A likely motive was revenge for the International Olympic Committee's decision to ban the Russian team from the Winter Games because of its history of doping violations (a practice that showed how ready Russia was to gain advantage by breaking the rules).[23]

The most important case of the use of social media, along with other methods, to influence a Western democracy was Russian support for Donald Trump during the 2016 presidential election campaign. This had a direct bearing on US policy toward Russia and Ukraine. The role of Russia in the election became the focus of an investigation by special counsel Robert S. Mueller III. In one indictment Evgeny Prigozhin, the sponsor of the Wagner group in Syria, was named as the founder of the Internet Research Agency, a St. Petersburg–based "troll farm." The agency appears to have been conceived during the 2011–12 protests against Putin's reelection, and was part of a wider effort geared to develop links with outside Far-Right and Far-Left groups that would be opposed to "globalization" and liberal interventionism. At its later peak the Internet Research Agency had an eighty-person team with specialists in graphics, data analysis, and search-engine optimization.

Mueller claimed that three Russians visited ten states in 2014, gathering intelligence about US politics. In February 2016 they were instructed to "use any opportunity to criticize Hillary [Clinton] and the rest (except Sanders and Trump—we support them.)" Social media was used to push out comments on the most divisive issues in American politics.[24] Another account suggests that the Russian effort was stepped up following the 2016 release of the Panama Papers—leaked documents from the files of a Panama-based law firm. The papers revealed that an old friend of Putin's, Sergey Roldugin, a classical cellist and conductor, had moved at least $2 billion through banks and offshore companies. He appeared to be acting as a front man for Putin loyalists, including possibly Putin himself.[25] This was more evidence that corruption was not only rife among Russia's elite but that Putin was a beneficiary, along with a collection of his comrades that went back to his old KGB days and his St. Petersburg (formerly Leningrad) connections. This was also an example of the extent to which Putin's group saw themselves as victims of information campaigns. He described the revelations as a conspiracy directed against the Russian people: "Our opponents are above all concerned by the unity and consolida-tion of the Russian nation. They are attempting to rock us from within, to make us more pliant." His spokesman described the allegations as the result of "Putinophobia" and pointed to "many former state department and CIA employees, as well as those of other intelligence services" in the journalistic consortium responsible for the revelations.[26] Almost immediately Putin is reported to have convened a meeting of his national security council and demanded some retaliation.[27]

During the course of 2016, the Russian effort was extensive. It included leaking stolen information, using Russian outlets to spread disinformation, and influencing social media debates with trolls and bots. Mueller named twelve Russian intelligence officers who had hacked into Democrats' emalls , using phishing techniques and transferred their haul to wikileaks. More than thirty thousand Russia-linked accounts generated 1.4 million tweets during final two months of the election campaign, using social media advertising (126 million people exposed to content tied to Russia-linked accounts over a two-year period), targeting voting systems, forging documents (including a crucial one that suggested collusion between Hillary Clinton and Attorney General Loretta Lynch)[28] Putin considered Clinton to have shown hostility in her support for the 2011 protests and disregard for Russian interests over Libya. Trump won because of deeper features of the US political system at the time and poor decisions made by the Clinton campaign. Analysis of the Russian effort suggested that the most effective items of "fake news" directed against Clinton originated in the US. Along with right-wing sites in the US, they were then accentuated and spread by Russians.[29]

One curiosity was that the Russians did not seem bothered that the Americans knew how much they were interfering, as if it were a signal on its own about their readiness to do to the Americans what the Americans had tried to do to them. The interference was hardly covert. The Obama administration was uncertain about how best to make public what was known on the assumption that Trump was going to lose, and it would be easier for Clinton to deal with the issue as president.[30] Obama worried that taking too strong a line might lead the Russians to dump even more explosive material while appearing as if the administration was trying to sway US opinion in favor of Clinton. A statement was issued on October 7, 2016, expressing the intelligence community's confidence that "the Russian Government directed the recent compromises of e-mails" from US political organizations.[31]

Purloined emails from the Democratic National Committee and the Democratic Congressional Campaign Committee were used as bait to make connections with the Trump campaign. But the Kremlin was also helped by key figures in the Trump campaign having close connections. Paul Manafort, for example, had worked for Yanukovych in his 2010 election campaign.[32] The unexpected result suggested that Putin's gamble in authorizing the effort had paid off. Relations with a Clinton administration were never going to be easy, but the evidence of Russian interference would have made them even worse. Once Trump was elected, it seemed reasonable to assume that there would be a sharp improvement in US-Russian relations, possibly to the detriment of Ukraine, especially as General Michael Flynn became Trump's national security advisor. However, the knowledge of Russian tampering with the 2016 election was now embedded within the institutions of American government and would not go away, especially as the FBI was starting to investigate how it had come about. Within weeks of Trump's inauguration, Flynn was out on the grounds of having misled the vice president.

THE TRUMP EFFECT

What difference did Trump make to American policy? When it came to Syria, President Obama had been convinced, on his own country's experience of Iraq and Afghanistan, that committing troops to counterinsurgency was a fool's game. He forecast that Putin would face a quagmire of his own.[33] He also belittled Putin's international role, insisting that despite his engagement in Crimea and Syria he was unable to set the international agenda at meetings of the G20. He did not accept that there was any link between his own inaction in Syria in 2013 and Russian action in Ukraine. Bush's engagement in Iraq, he noted, had not prevented the Russian invasion of Georgia. He was clear about the asymmetry of motivation. Ukraine was more important to Russia than to the US: "There are ways to deter," he observed, "but it requires you to be very clear ahead of time about what is worth going to war for and what is not." His view was that he had no reason to interrupt Russia while it was making a terrible mistake. "They are overextended. They're bleeding. And their economy has contracted for three years in a row, drastically." He did little to encourage the bleeding. Obama refused to provide "lethal" military equipment to Ukraine. Support was confined to armored vehicles, medical supplies, and night-vision goggles. Ukraine was denied capabilities they wanted, such as Javelin antitank missiles, antibattery radar, and advanced intelligence and communications capabilities. In 2015, the House of Representatives passed a resolution with a clear majority (348 to 48) to urge that defensive weapons be sent to Ukraine.

Some new political initiative was expected after January 2017 when Donald Trump was inaugurated as the forty-fifth president of the United States. As a candidate Trump spoke of the need for improved relations with Russia, and his representatives beat back efforts to have the Republican 2016 platform endorse lethal assistance to Ukraine.[34] But once in government Trump found it difficult to argue for a pro-Russian stance as he did not want to confirm the impression that he was Russia's puppet. His advisors did not share his pro-Russian stance, especially once Michael Flynn had been obliged to resign. Congressional and bureaucratic pressure moved toward providing lethal arms to Ukraine.[35] These were eventually authorized.[36]

The big issue was sanctions. If Putin had really staged a political coup in Washington then he would expect to see these eased or even removed. In late July 2017, in one of the first pieces of legislation passed by Congress under the new administration, a new sanctions resolution was sent to the president. Because it enjoyed bipartisan support, he was unable to veto the bill.[37] The proposed new sanctions would address a number of transgressions including Russian interference in the 2016 US election, its human rights violations, as well as its annexation of Crimea and its operations in Eastern Ukraine. The immediate Russian response to the bill was to demand that the US reduce the size of its diplomatic staff by 755 and banned the staff from using two properties. In response the US told Russia to close its San Francisco consulate and annexes in Washington and New York.[38] At the end of January 2018, however, when a deadline was reached for imposing new sanctions, the State Department announced that this would not happen, pointing to the continuing impact of previous sanctions, which were just starting to be felt, and the need to keep something in reserve as a deterrent.[39]

There was therefore ambiguity in the US system when it came to sanctions against Russia. On the one hand the president wanted to improve relations with Russia.[40] Yet there remained public support in the US for sanctions, as much because of allegations of Russian influence during the 2016 elections or even its support for President Assad in Syria as actions in Ukraine.[41] In the spring of 2018, two additional episodes pushed the Trump administration to more sanctions. The first was the response coordinated by Britain to the attempted murders of a former Russian agent Sergei Skripal and his daughter Yulia in Salisbury using nerve agents. Russia had dismissed the accusations, even suggesting that British intelligence was really responsible, combined with knowing observations that their fate should be a warning to other traitors. The US took the opportunity to expel some fifty Russian intelligence agents from the US. Then more sanctions were announced by the US ambassador to the United Nations in response to Russian support for a Syrian chemical weapons attack on rebels. In both cases Trump sought to mitigate the impact of announcements from his own administration. With the first set, it was later reported that Russia had been told that while these individuals must leave, they could be replaced. With the second set, Trump simply cancelled them.[42]

Then, with little warning, sanctions were imposed on twenty-four Russian oligarchs and officials, and on twelve related companies as a response to "worldwide malign activity." This time the impact was hard and immediate. A key figure on the list was Oleg Deripaska. Two companies he was associated with, including Rusal (a major producer of aluminum), lost half their value. The Russian market was now down 10 percent. These sanctions, more than any others, appeared to threaten the ability of Russian businesses to gain access to capital markets.[43] Of a variety of Russian countersanctions considered, one of the more serious was to block titanium and uranium sales.[44] A third of the titanium used by Boeing came from a Russian state monopoly.

There was soon a search for a compromise, this time lifting the sanctions on Rusal so long as Deripaska divested his holding.[45]

Trump's readiness to talk to Putin, which led to the Helsinki summit of July 2018, reflected his belief that he could do a deal with anyone. The main controversy at the summit was generated by Trump's support for Putin's reassurances in the face of hard evidence from the intelligence community that Russia had interfered in the 2016 election. There were reports of security deals, including on Ukraine, but as there were no formal records of the discussion between the two presidents it was hard to know the status of any agreements. The most substantial gain in foreign policy terms for Putin was Trump's consistent undermining of the Western alliance. The president had never shown much enthusiasm for NATO, and in 2018 he began a trade war, largely directed at China but which also involved imposing tariffs on Canada and the US's European allies for "national security reasons." There was little support in the public or congressional opinion for a move out of NATO, but the lack of agreement on a range of key foreign policy issues was evident, from climate change to Iran's nuclear program, and demands for a greater defense effort from Europeans, left Nato looking fragile.[46]

By this time Russia had been on the receiving end of sanctions and diplomatic slights for four years, ever since Crimea was annexed. Putin had managed to ride out the attempts to isolate and coerce Russia. The points of tension had moved beyond the issue connected to Ukraine, taking in now the measures taken by both sides in response to that crisis. There was talk of a new Cold War, with some familiar concerns reemerging: for example, about the ability of Russia to catch NATO unawares with a surprise conventional offensive, and the dangers of nuclear escalation. In all this, a sense of perspective was required. Russia was in a far weaker position than the Soviet Union had been. Its former allies in the Warsaw Pact, along with the Baltic States, were members of NATO. Moscow's "sphere of influence" had shrunk dramatically, which was one reason for its sense of isolation and insecurity. What used to be the Soviet Union was now the priority focus for its foreign and security policy: its "near abroad." It no longer had a global reach. Syria represented the limits of its power projection. Nor could Russia claim leadership of an international ideological movement. Its main messages were crudely nationalist, and so its natural supporters were on the xenophobic right of European politics. Most importantly, whereas the Soviet Union was, almost until its collapse, the second-largest economy in the world, Russia was at around twelfth or thirteenth place in the economic league table. Its GDP was about 60 percent that of France and the UK, 40 percent of Germany, and not even 8 percent of the United States. Russia's lack of economic pull meant that even when sympathetic leaders got to power, as in Hungary, Russia could not offer comparable economic support to the EU.

In such circumstances, rather than make direct challenges, it had to limit its liabilities. This had come to mean sticking with provocations just below the threshold that might lead to a hot war. Conflict was now conducted in a gray world of acts that were hard to attribute, and indeed often carried out by private individuals and groups acting as agents of the state. When critical information systems went down suddenly, affecting banking or the government bureaucracy, or when fake and inflammatory messages overwhelmed social media, the fact that these acts were Russia's responsibility could be hard to prove for sure. Responsibility was always denied, without much attempt to make the denials plausible, and often with a knowing sneer. Refusal to be accountable for actions was combined with an impression of deliberate menace. While China was increasing its economic clout and political influence, it was Russia that was drawing attention to itself. Yet the limits to its power remained profound. With this came a danger of overestimating Russia's capabilities while underestimating the sources of its own insecurities. Putin wanted to be talked up and not down. He wanted Russia to appear as a great power whose interests must be accommodated and have a say in all important issues. Yet in the end it was a minor economic power that had allowed its insecurities to lead it into behavior that could hurt its adversaries without doing much for the aspirations and needs of the Russian people.

UKRAINE

Against this backdrop of multiple tensions Ukraine became less important. The Russo-Ukraine conflict appeared to have reached a stable equilibrium. Neither side was prepared to make the effort to achieve a military breakthrough. Both had adjusted to its special demands. A "mutually hurting stalemate" is often seen to be as one ripe for a negotiated settlement.[47] Yet this does not mean that negotiations will take place or succeed. The hurt, while mutual, may also be quite manageable. In this case, there was no obvious improvement to be made to the underlying principles informing the February 2015 Minsk settlement. What it lacked was an enforcement mechanism and an agreed sequence for its implementation.

Both sides adapted to a conflict without an obvious end. In Ukraine there was frustration over the impasse, for it had lost territory which it wished to recover. But it could cope. Ukraine was generally recognized as the aggrieved party and was satisfied with the underlying principles behind the Minsk agreements without being tested on how their implementation would go about. It had no interest in a lesser agreement that would legitimize the Russian occupation.

The war took its toll. The immediate impact of the crisis on Ukraine's economy was catastrophic, and it continued to struggle under the weight of the expense and distractions of the war. After failing to grow in 2013, the economy went down by 6.8 percent in 2014 and another 12 percent in 2015, with a degree of recovery beginning only in 2016.[48] Although 4.8 percent growth was achieved in 2016, it fell back to 2 percent in 2017, far below what was required for a serious recovery. The economic difficulties were the result of lost production in occupied territory (including Crimea), lost trade with Russia, and, to a lesser extent, lost foreign direct investment.[49] Coal production fell by roughly two-thirds and steel production by a third because of the loss of mines and steel mills in the occupied areas. The separatists sold off key infrastructure. Exports to Russia were cut by half using illicit measures, despite Russia's membership in the World Trade Organization. Unsurprisingly, Russia showed no interest in debt relief, despite Ukraine's stricken finances.[50]

At the same time, Ukraine had to cope with the humanitarian crisis resulting from the war, including 1.3 million people internally displaced.[51] The war cost about $5 million a day. To transform the military into a serious fighting force, defense spending rose from about 2.5 percent of GDP in 2013 to about 5 percent at around $6 billion, including some $700 million in new procurement. International support was not generous, with the EU only providing some $5 billion, although progress was made with the International Monetary Fund (IMF) on debt relief.[52] The Ukrainian parliament, prodded by the IMF, adopted a number of reforms, including measures to reduce Ukraine's dependence on Russian gas and institute anticorruption laws.[53] The measures were painful, with energy subsidies and pensions cut.

On January 18, 2017, the Ukrainian parliament passed the Donbas De-Occupation Law. Russia was designated as an "aggressor state" and responsible for the damage caused as a result of fighting in the "temporarily occupied" enclaves.[54] A few weeks later a small group of Ukrainian irregulars and volunteers blocked rail traffic across the line of control. This halted freight between the separatist territories and the rest of Ukraine. Although the move was at first opposed by Poroshenko, it was popular, and he therefore turned it into a trade-and-energy blockade on the occupied territories. The separatists responded by seizing control of coal mines and steel and chemical plants owned by Rinant Akhmeoc, Ukraine's richest oligarch and biggest employer. From the start of the conflict it had suited both sides to allow Akhmeoc's businesses to carry on without regard for the dispute. Now fifty-six thousand miners lost their incomes.[55] This also had a knock-on effect on the wider Ukrainian economy.

Corruption remained high, if declining and not as well organized as before. At first, many ministers were young and Western-educated, and in government and Parliament the rhetoric was pro-European. But the old structures of power were resilient. The momentum behind Euromaidan was not sustained after the uprising. The activists were too diverse to form a single bloc with a clear message. There was no new administrative elite ready to take the place of the one that had served Yanukovych, although the old elite did at least keep the state functioning during the chaotic events of early 2014.[56] There were some positive developments, including reduced energy dependence on Russia, reform of the police force, and improvements to health care. Against this, many in entrenched positions of power in the police and judiciary showed no interest in modernizing. After a promising start, the effort to reform the economic and political system began to falter. Although the energy sector had become much cleaner, the surge in military spending opened up more possibilities for mismanagement and dubious deals. The old-guard politicians regained control of the government and resisted attempts to shift power away from the oligarchs and deal with corruption. After the National Anti-Corruption Bureau (NABU) arrested a deputy defense minister and the ministry's procurement chief, an attack began on NABU. Parliament drafted legislation, later dropped, which intended to undermine NABU. The domestic intelligence service even raided the homes of NABU employees.[57] According to Transparency International, Ukraine still competed with Russia to be the most corrupt country in Europe.[58]

Poroshenko appeared to see the challenge as doing enough to keep Western backers calm while avoiding real reform. He hoped that the position of his country as a victim of Russian aggression would shield his government from pressure. Concerns about corruption and the rule of law, however, badly affected investment and left the IMF unimpressed.[59] IMF officials left Kiev in November 2017 refusing to assure it of another aid tranche without more efforts to combat corruption.[60] As had been the case four years earlier, the IMF remained the most persistent source of pressure on reform. The difference this time was that the same message was coming from the EU, and Russia no longer offered a fallback position. Although numerous individuals were being investigated, fewer were being indicted or convicted. In June 2018 the Rada eventually passed legislation to establish an independent anti-corruption court to fill this evident gap in the system.[61]

A poll at the beginning of 2018 demonstrated that Ukrainians were as unhappy as ever about the direction in which their country was heading, and they had minimal respect for the country's politicians and political institutions. They still wanted to join the EU, although not as confidently as before, and still preferred Western countries to Russia, although they were less positive about everything. By far the biggest issue facing the country was corruption (48 percent), followed by military action in Donbas (42 percent). Concern about the Russian language was 1 percent.[62]

RUSSIA

When the crisis broke. Russia's economy was in a relatively strong position, although its position deteriorated quickly. The ruble was one of the worst performing currencies in 2014 and would have fallen further if reserves had not been used to prop it up. Credit ratings were downgraded. Inflation ran into double figures, well ahead of growth in wages and of the indexing of pensions. By the summer of 2015, the currency reserves accumulated during the good years of high commodity prices looked healthy at $360 billion, but they were still down from $500 billion at the start of 2014.[63]

If the economy had been reformed it would have been able to cope better, but little had been done to increase Russian competiveness and tackle corruption. Because of the tense international situation the military budget stayed supported while reserve funds were further depleted. Although growth recovered slightly in 2017, it was still weak into 2018; household incomes continued to decline.[64] With oil and natural gas still accounting for 60 percent of export revenue and 50 percent of the federal government's tax base, vulnerability to price fluctuations remained. The government coped with sanctions by limiting the support to the ruble and cutting the nonmilitary state budget. Although emergency capital was pumped into the banking system, it remained fragile. Investment was low, with would-be investors deterred not only by actual or prospective sanctions but also the confiscatory and corrupt nature of the Russian system.[65]

The combination of sanctions and the fall in the oil price did not bring the economy to its knees, but it hit the standard of living of ordinary Russians. Despite Russian efforts to encourage member states to vote against them, the sanctions imposed by the EU as a result of Crimea were reenacted every six months.[66] The G7, now without Russia, stated in its communiqué after its June 2015 summit:

> We recall that the duration of sanctions should be clearly linked to Russia's complete implementation of the Minsk agreements and respect for Ukraine's sovereignty. They can be rolled back when Russia meets these commitments. However, we also stand ready to take further restrictive measures in order to increase cost on Russia should its actions so require. We expect Russia to stop trans-border support of

separatist forces and to use its considerable influence over the separatists to meet their Minsk commitments in full.[67]

Despite the pressure put on Western countries to end the sanctions, they stuck to the line that they could not be concluded until Minsk was implemented. At the same time, because their effects could be managed, there were limits on their coercive value. Precisely because they were targeted, most Russians did not feel that the sanctions had much impact on their own lives.[68]

The prospect of more sanctions added to the pressure. Western financial institutions became warier of taking on Russian clients.[69] The most severe sanction was held in reserve. This was kicking Russia out of the Society for Worldwide Interbank Financial Telecommunication (SWIFT) system through which organizations and countries access the international financial system.[70] The severity of this potential sanction was evident in the concern shown by Russians, to the extent of describing it as being tantamount to an act of war. Medvedev promised to "watch developments and if such decisions [to restrict access to SWIFT] are made, I want to note that our economic reaction and generally any other reaction will be without limits."[71]

Early on in the conflict there were claims that Russia would reduce its dependence on Western markets by looking to Asia.[72] A closer partnership with China could be a geopolitical "game changer."[73] China shared Russia's desire to limit American predominance in the international system, and shared its preference for authoritarian systems and dislike of interference in internal affairs (although on this latter matter it also noted Russia's inconsistency). But China took advantage of Russia's weakness to achieve attractive deals on oil supplies. It was content for Russia to seek to get closer to offset its deteriorating relations with the West, but gave no sign of being prepared to do Moscow any economic favors. Trade declined from 2014 to 2015 and little was done on proposed new oil pipelines. Any investments were the result of competitive prices as much as a geopolitical calculation.[74] By and large Russia lacked the strong technology and services sectors that attracted Chinese funds. It certainly did not feel that relations with Russia required it to discriminate against Ukraine in its economic relations. Ukraine became the largest corn exporter to China.[75] It has invested significantly in Ukrainian transportation and agriculture.[76]

For Russia, the conflict added costs not only in the extra spending allocated to the armed forces but also in the subventions required by the enclaves and by Crimea. The additional cost of Crimea was put at $4–5 billion per year. For the people of Crimea, life became more difficult after annexation because of the problems of keeping it supplied and sustaining the economy.[77] A bridge across the Kerch Strait to provide a direct link to Russia was eventually completed in 2018. So important is this bridge that considerable efforts went into securing it against a range of possible threats.[78]

For the longer term, the key question for Russia was the future of its energy sector. This was at the same time a potent source of leverage but also a vital source of revenue.[79] This explains the hurt when the price of oil was cut in half in 2014 and the importance of the later recovery in the price. But it was also affected by measures taken by its customers to reduce dependence on Russian supplies. Ukraine and Lithuania reduced direct gas imports from Russia by means of "reverse flows." Gas still came from Russia, but it went to Slovakia, Hungary, and Poland where it was intermingled with gas from Norway and Holland, and then moved back—from west to east—to Ukraine and Lithuania. With less direct connection between Gazprom and the supply to individual countries, the old systems of rewards and punishments were undermined. New pipelines and liquefied natural gas (LNG) terminals, including in Lithuania and Poland, allowed for imports from other suppliers.

In March 2018 there was a test of these measures. An arbitration concluded that Russia's Gazprom owed the Ukrainian gas company Naftogaz after defaulting on its shipment obligations. Damages of $4.63 billion were awarded, which were reduced to $2.5 billion once payments for gas delivered were subtracted. By way of revenge Gazprom decided not to supply gas to Ukraine in March, creating shortages equivalent to 10 percent of daily consumption at a time of extremely cold weather. In response, Ukraine switched power plants from gas to fuel oil and asked schools, universities, and kindergartens to suspend lessons for a couple of days.[80]

The controversies around Ukraine, sanctions, and Russia's past tendency to use energy supplies as an instrument of pressure also had an impact on two large pipeline projects. The South Stream project was an early casualty of the conflict. This was to take gas across the Black Sea to the Balkans and on to Italy and Austria. Getting support for this project was a major focus of Russian efforts in Hungary and Bulgaria, including support for their governments and promised discounts on their gas. The difficulty was that they required the European Commission to agree to exemptions from those European energy and competition policies with which Russia would not comply. Prior to

February 2014 there were indications of potential compromises
and even a possibility that the value of the project would lead to
the Commission being ignored. In late March, after Crimea's annexation, the Commission suspended negotiations. In December,
Putin abandoned the project on the grounds that it would no
longer be profitable. This was an interesting example of the limits
of Russian influence. Many Russian companies were engaged
with the Bulgarian economy while Hungarian prime minister
Viktor Orbán made little secret of his sympathies with Russia. In
the end, however, both these countries needed EU funds to keep
their economies afloat.[81]

This left the North Stream as the most important link between Russian energy and the West. North Stream 1 supplied
more than 50 percent of Germany total gas consumption, and
the German government was ready (despite otherwise insisting
on full implementation of agreed economic sanctions) to continue with North Stream 2. The Germans had limited their alternative energy options by deciding to abandon nuclear power.
The new pipelines would result in gas arriving via the Baltic
Sea, bypassing Poland, Ukraine, and the Baltic States. Ukraine
would be left more vulnerable as it would mean that gas transit
through the country would be unnecessary. Poland lobbied extensively against the plan, but Germany insisted that this had
to be largely seen as a business venture. Denmark, Sweden, and
Finland were less sure.[82] Chancellor Merkel was caught between
the contrasting economic and political logic of the scheme. When
speaking with Poroshenko she said that the project would not go
ahead if it left Ukraine "in the lurch" and acknowledged that the
project was more than a business deal. Nonetheless, Germany issued all the permits needed for the pipe to be laid in German

waters.[83] The European Commission, however, remained concerned about Gazprom's anticompetitive practices within the European market, a number of which were exposed in an internal document published in April 2018. An annex to the report detailed how Gazprom used destination clauses, reexport bans, restrictions on metering stations, and refusals to change delivery points to "segment" the EU states.[84]

Putin's strategy was described as being one of "hunkering down and playing for time," waiting for oil prices and the ruble to recover so that he could continue with his geopolitical priorities.[85] In a speech directed to the West in St. Petersburg in June 2015, the president reminded his audience of warnings that there would be a "deep crisis." Instead, he observed, Russia has "stabilized the situation . . . mainly because the Russian economy piled up a sufficient supply of inner strength."[86] The official narrative portrayed a country under attack from the West, with every blow traced back to an American initiative. The spirit of the Second World War was constantly invoked, encouraging a militarization of Russian culture. Putin's poll ratings suggested that this approach resonated with the Russian people. One report had stratospheric 89 percent approval rating,[87] higher than the 64 percent who said that they approved of the country's direction.[88] He had assumed the role of tsar, above politics, a supreme authority to whom the masses could appeal in troubled times, but also to a conviction that with the Sochi Olympics and the annexation of Crimea, he had restored Russia's international standing.[89]

The overall picture was still less of a great power ascendant and more of one struggling to cope with a set of reversals.[90] In March 2018 Putin was reelected for another six years (the presidential term had been extended from four to six years). As serious opposition figures had been barred from standing for election, his victory was never in doubt. His nightmare remained a color revolution of his own that would prove impossible to contain.

In a June 2015 interview with an Italian newspaper, Putin had insisted on Russia's modest ambition:

> All our actions, including those with the use of force, were aimed not at tearing away this territory from Ukraine but at giving the people living there an opportunity to express their opinion on how they want to live their lives.

He described the implementation of the Minsk agreements in terms of ensuring "the autonomous rights of the unrecognized republics," which would give them the "right to speak their language, to have their own cultural identity and engage in cross border trade." This would require a law on municipal elections and an amnesty. Instead, he lamented, Ukraine was not prepared to have such a conversation, hence the deadlock. Even worse, the Ukrainian government has "simply cut them off from the rest of the country. They discontinued all social payments—pensions, benefits; they cut off the banking system, made regular energy supply impossible, and so on."[91]

One complication for Putin was the requirement that separatist leaders cooperated with any deal. Yet they remained wary about a political process that could put their own positions under threat. They were not simply puppets, although they owed their positions to Moscow and could not last without Russian support. Foreign Minister Sergei Lavrov acknowledged Moscow's influence with the separatists, but he also insisted that it was not "as great as 100 percent."[92] Separatist leaders asserted their wish to be wholly independent of Ukraine and preferably part of Russia, even though the Minsk agreements gave no support for these possibilities. Any idea of re-creating the old Novorossiya was lost with Minsk. While militarily the territories could be held, economic and social conditions within became difficult. There were reports of shortages, discontent, and criminality. The governments were immature, unstable, and suffered from power struggles. Significant numbers of men were under their command, but training and discipline often appeared poor, and, as is often the case with militias, they could soon become indistinguishable from gangsters.[93] One authoritative account described them as being "primarily comprised" of Russian mercenaries, intelligence and military personnel, marginalized locals from economically distressed areas, radical groups from Russia and the former Soviet Union, including Cossack bands, Russian Orthodox Christian radicals, Russian nationalists, and Communists, sports hooligans, and defectors from Ukrainian security forces. They were disorganized, factionalized, rarely working "effectively with each other on the battlefield," often engaged in "rampant criminality, particularly theft, smuggling, extortion, and violent assault", and suffering from "pervasive substance abuse." The Kremlin's frustration with the local leadership and also with commanders with little local following led to regular purges.[94] Igor Strelkov (who had his own axe to grind) described these formations as more "mercenary than militia," likely to collapse within forty-eight hours without Russian support.[95] They were kept going because Russia could not let them fail. Men and material could pass back and forth across the border and could be reinforced by regular units in the event of a crisis.

Along with other territories in Georgia and Moldova, Donetsk and Luhansk were in a state of limbo, neither part of one state or another, run as independent entities by local leaders who lacked popular legitimacy. From early on it had been apparent that Russia had been unable to find credible figures to run the enclaves. Those who had come to the fore often barely knew each other and lacked any administrative experience. They soon understood that they were not trusted by Russia. One leader was reported as describing the enclaves as a burden for Russia, "like a suitcase without a handle: you can't use it, but you don't want to throw it out."[96]

Luhansk in particular appeared to be subject to inner turmoil: examples of this were a thwarted coup attempt in September 2016 involving a number of senior political figures, and the murder of the defense minister by a car bomb in February 2017. In November 2017 armed men appeared in a confrontation between Igor Plotnitsky, the head of the "Republic," and his interior minister, Igor Kornet, which led to Plotnitsky resigning for "health reasons" (which appeared to be war wounds) and fleeing to Russia. The security minister, Leonis Pasechnik, became the new leader and pledged support for Minsk, suggesting that the Russians were looking for a more compliant local leadership.

To some extent the deadlock suited Moscow because it put off the day when Ukraine reasserted sovereignty over its own territory. By keeping up the pressure it was hard for Ukraine to get even closer to the European Union or consider joining NATO. For their own reasons, both institutions would be careful before they granted Ukraine a formal status, although both stepped up informal connections and provided practical support. But neither was Ukraine in a hurry to implement Minsk. The Novorossiya project, which in principle could have covered nine out of the twenty-four regions of Ukraine, was defunct. The Ukrainian economy was adapting to the loss of Donetsk and Luhansk. Even if a new constitution was agreed with more decentralization to satisfy the Minsk conditions, in any all-Ukraine elections, the separatists were likely to do poorly. As Ukrainian forces improved, helped by Western advisors, they put the separatist forces under pressure. They repulsed assaults on their positions and made some tactical advances. By and large, however, the front lines barely changed.

In September 2017 Putin appeared interested in breaking the deadlock by proposing a peacekeeping force. The idea was not new. Poroshenko had proposed a UN peacekeeping force to carry out the cease-fire that had been agreed in Minsk.[97] This would have potentially involved a direct intervention in the fighting. Putin's proposal was to introduce peacekeepers along the line of contact separating Ukraine from the enclaves. This line was 400 kilometers (248.5 miles) long, although the focus of Putin's proposal was the operational area along this line, which was only 6 kilometers (3.6 miles). It would have a limited mandate to protect the OSCE monitors. All this proposal would achieve would be a frozen conflict.[98]

Putin's proposal did start a debate on where a peacekeeping force could play a useful role. The obvious alternative was the true Russia-Ukraine border. Such a peacekeeping force would have to be substantial, though, perhaps as many as fifty thousand strong, and would oversee Russia's withdrawal of its people (supposing they could be identified) and heavy weapons, and the militias disbanding. If this alternative had any attraction for Russia it lay in ruling out Ukrainian forces and police entering the territories during the transition period. This would reduce the risk of reprisals as displaced people were encouraged to return to their homes, and industrial and agricultural production was restored. An interim civilian administration that possessed a credible governance and criminal justice system would also allow for a more gradual return of Ukrainian institutions. Eventually secure elections would unlock other aspects of Minsk. While there were signs of Ukraine and Russia "groping for a way to dial down the violence" there was no real momentum behind these efforts.[99]

In November 2017 the Office of the UN High Commissioner for Human Rights reported, "In total, from April 14, 2014, to November 15, 2017, the OHCHR recorded 35,081 conflict-related casualties in Ukraine among Ukrainian armed forces, civilians and members of the armed groups. This includes 10,303 people killed and 24,778 injured." It cautioned that this was a conservative estimate. The data was incomplete "due to gaps in coverage of certain geographic areas and time periods, and due to overall underreporting, especially of military casualties. Injuries have been particularly underreported."[100] While civilian casualties were at a low level compared to earlier stages in the war when shelling caused more deaths, there were still sufficiently deadly items around, from mines, booby traps, and improvised explosive devices (IEDs), along with the "explosive remnants of war (ERW)." During the course of the conflict there had been many reports of "summary executions, enforced disappearances, arbitrary detention, torture and ill-treatment, and conflict-related sexual violence." Over time the situation had deteriorated, especially in Donetsk and Luhansk, as citizens lost their pensions and could get little or no restitution or compensation for property damaged or destroyed by the conflict. "These conditions," noted the OHCHR, "deepen the divide, jeopardize social cohesion and complicate prospects and efforts for future reconciliation." This led to "increasing manifestations of intolerance, including threats of violence, by extreme right-wing groups, which served to stifle public expressions and events by individuals holding alternative, minority social or political opinions. Violent acts which occurred remained largely unsanctioned." This was not a "frozen" conflict. It continued to take lives and ruin others.

Evaluation

Ukraine and the Art of Strategy

Strategy is about creating power. It is about making the most of available resources, achieving more than comparisons of relative strength might suggest would be possible. The Russo-Ukraine conflict provides more examples of bad strategy than of good. This is a story of situations made worse, with moves that failed to achieve what was intended or else resulted in unintended and damaging consequences.

The biggest failures were Russian. Vladimir Putin prized the shock value of a bold move as against a realistic assessment of how events might play out over the long term. Russian strategic thought is often assumed to be influenced by chess, a game in which it is necessary to think several moves ahead of the opponent, yet in Putin's case his strategic thought appears to be more influenced by Judo, a game which he played (earning a black belt) and follows closely. As Kimberley Marten observes, "Judo is about immediate tactics, not long-term strategy." A judoka, she notes, "sizes up the opponent, probes for their weaknesses, and tips the other off-balance in a flash—causing the opponent to fall from their own weight." To win it is not necessary to be "bigger or stronger than the opponent, just quicker and shrewder." The goal is to survive, to be sure "to be the last one standing at the end of the tournament, come what may."[1] But sometimes opponents cannot be tipped and they manage to keep their balance.

THE FALLACY OF THE DECISIVE FIRST MOVE

Historically, the fallacy of the decisive first move has been a regular source of bad military strategy.[2] It has meant that wars have been started that then turned out to be difficult to conclude. Expectations that an opponent caught off guard would crumble quickly were based on either assumptions of military weakness or a stressed society. Such expectations have often been dashed by enemies capable of holding out for some time—because they have forces left in reserve, irregulars able to sustain a different sort of struggle, and allies who will act to prevent their defeat. Over the course of a long conflict, people adapt to new circumstances. Social and economic life continues, even if impoverished compared to what was enjoyed before. Wars starting with resounding opening victories can therefore be very difficult to close out with formal surrenders and political demands met. A strategy of exhaustion is what is left when the possibilities for quick fixes have run out and the struggle has become one of endurance to see which side decides to give up first and cut its losses. With a total commitment exhaustion can set in quickly; with a limited commitment a fight can be sustained long past the point when it can be readily recalled why it began in the first place.

If something can be taken of significant value in the early stages of a conflict, then that may be sufficient, leaving one party satisfied and waiting until the opponent gives up trying to get it back out of frustration. If the Russo-Ukraine conflict had been purely about Crimea, for example, then Putin might have been able to congratulate himself on a job well done, cope with sanctions of limited effect, and then perhaps offer some conciliatory gestures to formalize the transfer of sovereignty. This might have followed the example of India when it annexed the Portuguese colony Goa in 1961. But that was not enough because the core issue involved Ukraine's overall political trajectory. Putin's preference would have been to coerce the new government in Ukraine so that it abandoned its drive for an ever-closer association with the EU, just as he had coerced its predecessor. Alternatively he might have encouraged further fragmentation of the country. But the success of Crimea was not repeated in Donbas. The enclaves of Donetsk and Luhansk were not self-sufficient, and Ukraine adapted to their loss over time, without ever accepting that this loss should be permanent.

The idea of strategists setting down objectives and then asking how they might be reached rarely matches the reality. It is more common for strategy in practice to begin with trying to work out how to solve a pressing problem with the resources at hand before moving on to review options and even then redefining the problem as the situation develops. This is what it means to act strategically. Instead of working back from the final destination, acting strategically means recognizing the limits set by the available options and considering how much they offer a plausible route to a more desirable state of affairs—if not the most desired. The strategist may have to make do with a state of affairs that barely represents an improvement over the starting situation.

Another problem with standard models of strategy making is that these models assume time for careful deliberation, with relevant information gathered for a full appreciation of the situation, interest clarified, and objectives set, and all options assessed against these objectives. Decision making, however, is often rushed, based on guesses and prejudices, and leaving much to chance and later improvisation. When an opponent takes the initiative, there may be little to do other than defend as best as possible and hope to be able to cope for a sufficient enough time to develop measures to retrieve the situation. Euromaidan meant that there was a long buildup, but the moment of crisis came abruptly with Yanukovych's sudden flight. This was why the Kremlin's decision making was hurried, caught in a rush of events for which only limited contingency planning had been possible.

No attempt was made to deter Russian action against Ukraine. At the time there was barely a government in Kiev, and so it was in no position to issue deterrent threats. Events had moved so quickly that neither the US nor the EU had begun to think about what might happen next. Nor was Ukraine covered by NATO's Article 5. Even if the US and its allies had not been taken by surprise by the Russian move into Crimea it is not evident what they could have said in advance to deter Moscow other than to say that this would be viewed with the "utmost seriousness" and lead to "grave consequences." They could not know themselves, speculatively, what sort of response they could arrange, and whether whatever they could put together would have made any difference to Moscow's calculations.

By its quick action, Moscow was able to catch everybody else by surprise, but that also meant that it did not have a chance to deter itself—that is, it had not thought through how the resulting crisis might unfold, and in particular whether it could secure the gains to make what it probably assumed to be limited costs (modest economic sanctions and diplomatic pressure) worthwhile. Russia struggled not because it was punished but because it made less of an impact on Ukraine than it intended. Russia was denied the progress it hoped to make rather than punished for the progress it did make.

DOING NOTHING OR SOMETHING

One of the hardest things to decide is to do nothing. This is obviously the case in the face of adverse developments, for doing nothing suggests indifference and implies helplessness. Yet a demand to do "something" may lead to actions that bring limited benefits and are counterproductive. If "something" is required, then a wise course may be to make the minimum early commitment to allow time to assess alternative courses of action and develop new options. At the same time, of course, the opponent may be doing the same thing, and might identify and then close off some of the more promising options.

There was no obligation on Moscow to respond to Euromaidan. Putin could have waited to see how events unfolded before making any irrevocable move. His "something" might have been no more than an assertion of Russia's concerns, especially for those in the south and east of the country, and a reminder of the importance of Russia to Ukraine's economic well-being. He might have given time for a new government to establish itself and seek some sort of accommodation. To keep up the pressure he might have issued an ultimatum demanding that Russia's interests be respected. Contacts would have been made to Western capitals to explain the inherent risks in the situation and urging that messages be passed on to Kiev. In these ways he could have gained time and kept his options open. But both Putin and Lavrov claimed that the situation was truly urgent, focusing on the announced repeal of the 2012 language law, though within days this move had been vetoed by the acting president. The first action taken was in Crimea, where Russians were unlikely to be at risk from hostile Ukrainian actions for some time, if ever. Seizing control of Crimea moved the "something" from an assertion of interest and concern, which might have been a largely symbolic gesture in its immediate effect, into a transformative act. Whatever the next steps taken, Russia had changed its own stakes and moved the conflict with Ukraine to a new level.

The contrast between Russia's ambitious first moves and the cautious Western response was striking. The EU was late in paying attention to the developing tensions between Ukraine and Russia. Its own internal differences meant that as the crisis developed it could not move far away from established policy until there was more certainty. When certainty came the situation was one for which there had been neither intellectual nor practical preparation. It is not unusual for liberal democracies to be distracted, risk-averse, and superficial when assessing developing situations. They then appear at a loss when they are caught by surprise. Authoritarian governments have a natural advantage when it comes to moving with speed and stealth, especially when there is no need for a major mobilization. It is not, however, invariably the case that a bold, quick action produces better outcomes than those that emerge out of a period of dithering and muddle. The slower decision may have been tested and explored more thoroughly. The real difficulty was that there was no readily available option that could be agreed by the US and EU and still avoid selling out Ukraine completely or risking an even deeper confrontation with Russia.

It soon became apparent that there was no half-option with Crimea, along South Ossetian or Transnistrian lines. These held no attractions for Russia or the local population. Once Crimea had been detached from Ukraine, it had to be placed in Russia. The precedent then influenced all aspects of the subsequent conflict between the two countries. It created expectations for the separatists and those who might have opposed Euromaidan but had no desire to be part of Russia. Taking the most pro-Russian region out of Ukraine meant that Russia was even less well-placed to resist a westward move in Ukrainian politics.

At first Ukraine had little strategy. Even if a course of action could have been agreed there was little capacity to see it through. There were moves that might have secured Crimea or at least made a Russian takeover difficult, but no orders were given and little could be done against a determined Russian response. In Eastern Ukraine, the early resistance to separatism came from Euromaidan supporters, nationalist militias, and local oligarchs, acting on their own volition. If the separatists had enjoyed the same sort of support that they did in Crimea, then Ukraine would have fragmented. The Rada's decision to repeal the language law came at a crucial moment and reinforced the view that the uprising was deeply Russophobic. By the time it was vetoed the damage had been done, although not as much as would have been the case if there had been no veto. The inability of the separatists to consolidate their positions, the lack of any serious mainstream opposition following the flight of Yanukovych and the collapse of his party, combined with the shock of the loss of Crimea, then provided both time and impetus for the interim government to establish itself, begin to fight back, and organize elections for a new president. Until the elections there was bound to be a question mark against the legitimacy of the government; following the elections this ceased to be an issue. The importance of this step now tends to be taken for granted but both Obama and Merkel demanded that it not be disrupted. Although there was no voting in the enclaves this was a red line that Russia respected.

After easily beating Tymoshenko, Poroshenko as president was able to garner international support and push forward with the (misnamed) "antiterrorist operation." There was a brief period when Ukraine was able to mount an offensive in the early summer of 2014. There are questions about the crude methods used against the separatist strongholds, which added to the misery of residents and their alienation from Kiev, and whether different approaches might have undermined separatist positions without pushing Moscow into a desperate defense. The determination to push hard against the separatists while the opportunity was there meant that the Ukrainian effort was uncoordinated and opportunistic. When Russian forces entered in numbers, Ukrainian forces struggled to cope, and tactical decision making was often poor.

Western countries stayed well clear of the fighting. The response to Crimea's annexation was limited economic sanctions and efforts to isolate Russia diplomatically. This was not because of any expectation that these measures would force Russia to abandon Crimea but as a means of repudiating the seizure of another's territory. It would have been surprising if the sanctions had caused Moscow to abandon a game that it was already playing for high stakes, and in the end the actual coercive effects were limited. But failing to react at all to a Russian intervention on this scale would have alarmed other countries in Russia's neighborhood who would have seen themselves next in line.[3] It would have been cited as evidence that the US was giving up on its leadership role and that the European Union was paralyzed. Yet more direct measures, such as military assistance, would have been seen as provocative in Moscow. At the same time they may well have been wasted as Ukrainian forces would have been unable at that time to take advantage. The US could, however, have left the issue open. By precluding the transfer of "lethal" equipment as a matter of principle it lost one potential diplomatic lever for the future. Little could be done at the UN because of the Russian veto on any Security Council resolution it did not like. In the end, therefore, all that was done by the US and the EU was to send a signal of concern combined with an implication that more might be done if the situation worsened.

One reason for tentative first steps is to ascertain the seriousness of the situation and the stakes involved. This is not very difficult when sovereign territory or a way of life is under direct threat. But situations can often be ambiguous and of uncertain relevance with features and repercussions that cannot be anticipated in advance. The impact of tougher measures can be appreciated only in the context of all else that is going on at the time, including crises that are of far greater salience and must take priority, or economic conditions that restrict options to those that are not too expensive. Once a commitment is made to even minimalist action, however, then a political stake is created in a conflict even while little is being done to influence its course. It can therefore be hard to keep to the minimum, and if that remains the decision, then the consequence may be to fail to meet stated objectives. This was the fate of the US with regard to Syria. In this case the ability of Ukrainian forces to contain the problem, at least once the Russians decided not to push harder militarily after February 2015, meant that the West could keep their support at a relatively low level. If the only available means for "solving" a problem are high-risk and carry few prospects of success, then the safe conclusion may be that this is a problem that must be managed without ever being "solved."

At the core of the Russia-Ukraine conflict was a struggle over territory. At least during the conflict's first year that was how progress by both sides was measured. Beyond the territory in contention, though, there was little agreement about what this conflict was about. For Ukraine it was about its core identity and the direction of its economic and foreign policy. For Putin it was originally about his project for the creation of a Eurasian Customs Union that could provide some compensation for the loss of the Soviet Union and a counter to the EU. There was soon an escalation in claims about what was actually at stake. Consider some of the accusations made during the first few months of this crisis: Russia alleged that there had been a fascist coup, supported by the West, putting ethnic Russians in Ukraine at risk, while annexing Crimea was no more than support for self-determination, confirmed by a referendum. The West argued that the referendum was suspect and that the annexation was a fundamental breach of international law, setting precedents for interventions wherever there were Russian communities. As the crisis intensified, Russia talked alarmingly about nuclear war and began to harass NATO members. In response, NATO began to speak of a renewed Russian threat and made plans to beef up core capabilities and provide additional protection. As the extent of Russian "information operations" became apparent, especially those conducted in 2016 in the US, then the issue became one of subversion of Western political processes. Putin's concern from the start had been that all Western efforts, from democracy promotion to the enlargement of NATO and the EU, were directed at subverting Russian political processes. Amid all these claims and counterclaims, there was enough raw material to provide justifications for actions far more severe than anything actually considered or implemented. There was a striking contrast between the notionally high stakes and the limited commitments, between the rhetorical specters on the one hand and the modest advances made by either side on the ground and the inertia surrounding the implementation of Minsk on the other. This was because much of the talk of how the conflict might escalate was intended to have a deterrent effect, to warn of the consequences of pushing the conflict to a new level. In the process, however, new rationales for action were developed and strategic interests redefined.

In the light of all this, was Russian strategy really so innovative? And, if it was, can it be considered successful? There were regular references to "hybrid warfare," which eventually came to be extended by NATO and the EU to include "information warfare" undertaken quite independently of military action. An early 2013 speech by Valery Gerasimov, chief of Russia's general staff, is normally cited as the most authoritative description of the Russian approach to hybrid warfare, although it was largely a reflection on American practice and recent conflicts in the Middle East. "New information technologies," he noted, could play an important role. As a result "frontal clashes of major military formations . . . are gradually receding into the past." They now involve "the broad use of political, economic, informational, humanitarian and other non-military measures." All of this, Gerasimov said, could be supplemented by firing up the local populace as a fifth column and by "concealed" armed forces.[4] From Moscow's perspective this was an approach in which the West was accomplished.[5]

There was a retrospective element to all of this.[6] The strategy that Russia eventually followed appeared to fit this approach, but in many respects it was improvised. This was no planned test of a new military theory. Samuel Charap notes that Donbas was one of the few places where any Russian-backed insurgency had any chance of prospering because of the language and cultural ties across the border to Russia as well as the ease of access.[7] In Ukraine the irregulars were expected to take the lead, but on their own, once they faced a serious opposition, they were pushed back. They depended on regular Russian forces to sustain them, regain what they had lost, and then deter any Ukrainian offensives. There was little to suggest that the Russians had hit upon a novel way to bring together regulars and irregulars, especially—as in this case—when the irregulars were themselves combinations of mercenaries, adventurers, and local militants.

In the summer of 2014 Russia might have cut its losses by continuing with its claim that the enclaves reflected a worthy and spontaneous local uprising for which it had no responsibility. It could have concentrated on the humanitarian issues raised by the crushing of a rebellion and arranging self-passage out of the combat zones. Instead, as Putin dared not let people who had apparently rallied to a Russian cause fail spectacularly, he doubled up on his commitment. Rather than irregulars reinforcing the regulars, the regulars were backing up the irregulars. They were always too disparate and poorly coordinated to constitute a cohesive and effective force. It is challenging enough to meld together different units of the same army, for example special forces and infantry battalions, but even more difficult where the forces coming together not only have different military tasks and methods but also distinct command structures and diverging political interests. Even among the militia groups in Donetsk and Luhansk there were differences. As conditions became harsher within those areas, these differences grew. Some groups moved away from politics and into criminality. At the same time, Ukrainian forces also saw awkward combinations of militias and regular forces.[8]

There was nothing particularly complicated about the strategies employed in the fighting or what made the difference. For both sides, territorial gains depended on the application of superior military force. The separatists were stronger to start with in the spring of 2014 and created the enclaves. Then the Ukrainians were stronger and made inroads into the enclaves, until the Russians backed the separatists more overtly and pushed the Ukrainians back again. The force was rarely employed with great subtlety, with artillery barrages often the tactic of choice. Moreover, Russian efforts to deny their own direct involvement limited the forces that they could deploy. This was especially the case with air power. The Ukrainian Air Force was in a decrepit state in 2014. In the most intensive months of the fighting it lost some eighteen aircraft (ten helicopters and eight fixed-wing) to either shoulder-fired rocket launchers or surface-to-air missiles.[9] After that they largely relied on drones for reconnaissance purposes. Although there was talk at times of the separatists developing their own air forces nothing much materialized. As it demonstrated in Syria, the Russian Air Force could have made a deadly difference to the balance of forces, but no denials of Russian involvement could then have been made. A decision to end all pretense and overrun Ukraine would have involved Russia using all its regular forces. Against this the Ukrainians would have struggled, but as the early experience in Eastern Ukraine demonstrated, this would not have been seen as an act of liberation, and the more territory occupied, the longer the supply lines and the more hostile the local population.

The war was limited because Russia was not prepared to push forward with its regular forces, but instead it sought to sustain the enclaves until such time as some deal could be agreed upon. It put on and maintained a strong show of strength on its side of the border. The aim might have been to coerce Kiev into implementing Minsk on Russian terms, but it might also have had a deterrent function, encouraging Kiev not to mount offensives of its own. The regular exchanges of fire, in addition to keeping otherwise bored troops busy, also had the function of demonstrating that nothing had yet been settled. The references to nuclear forces also had a deterrent function. It was important for Russia to exude a sense of menace to make sure that others treated it with care and respect.

Dima Adamsky has cautioned that the West's focus on "hybrid war" does not fully capture the Russian discourse. He describes a Russian form of "cross-domain coercion" that "expands the continuum of options on the escalation ladder while minimizing the scale of kinetic operating." It provides a way of promoting interests while avoiding major war by "shaping and manipulating the strategic behavior of its adversaries using a repertoire of tools without employing massive brute force." Adamsky also notes that this approach can struggle to signal intent and interest. Russian messages did not always get through, and indeed were misunderstood.[10] The "nonkinetic" aspects of this campaign were the most innovative, but did they provide Moscow with any sort of strategic breakthrough?

The purpose of any information campaign is to support a particular narrative—either about the evil and perfidy of the enemy and the virtues of one's own side, or, more indirectly, to influence political trends in relevant countries by supporting one party's claims as against others (for example about the consequences of extensive migration or the untrustworthiness of a particular candidate).[11] These narratives cannot be created out of thin air. They must fit in with realities on the ground or existing prejudices. Thus displays of military strength were geared to shaping a narrative around Russia's strength. Because Putin was seen as a model for nationalist, authoritarian political leadership in Europe, those who wished to emulate him readily followed his statements and claims.

There is no evidence that the cleverest information campaign can shape events without something to work on. It is still difficult to win the narrative battle when losing the physical one on the ground. Successful "narratives" could not be constructed at random. Russia could not sustain claims that separatists were acting entirely on their own. It undermined further its credibility with the series of increasingly specious explanations for the downing of the MH-17 airliner.[12] By constantly denying its role, Russia introduced a huge complication into the conduct of the war and the associated diplomacy. If the intention was to spread an invisibility cloak over military preparations and operations, this effort failed.[13] The Kremlin's fiction might have initially facilitated the Russian intervention, but it also became a restriction. Its wider consequences include a growing distrust of all Russian government pronouncements, at least outside of Russia. This was evident following the Salisbury "nerve agent" incident in the UK, when chemical weapons were used in an attempted assassination. Despite attempts to explain away the attacks, accusing the British government of lying, Russia found itself facing coordinated action from more than twenty countries, leading to the expulsion of over one hundred intelligence agents. Not only was the UK able to provide intelligence to back up its claims and refute those of Russia, but most Western countries were weary of years of outrageous Russian claims and deceptions.

The natural corollary was an increased authoritarianism in Russia and a clampdown on domestic news outlets and independent organizations that might challenge the official line. It is easier to fabricate and dissemble when the local media has been turned into government mouthpieces and dissent squashed. But there are risks for a government when it relies on implausible claims that do not match the actual experience of its target audience. Once this is noticed its credibility is lost, and it may not be believed even when telling the truth.

When the claims did ring true to the target audience, then the ability to amplify and spread them through energetic use of social media could make a difference. This might be extremely significant, for example, in helping Trump win an election and the Leave campaign in the UK's referendum on membership in the EU. But making a difference is not the same as gaining a lasting political dividend. That still depends on wider factors of power and interests. There are reasons to be concerned with the stresses and strains within NATO and the EU and to note the extent that the fragmentation of either would serve Russian interests. The reasons for Brexit or Trump's election lie in developments in the internal politics of the UK and the US, even though the extent to which Russia was able to give them a nudge is troubling. Moscow can also be expected to continue with its information campaigns and cyberattacks, not least because they are inexpensive and the occasional success may make a much larger effort worthwhile. Yet these campaigns also carry risks for Russia. As its methods are exposed this irritates the targets and embarrasses the beneficiaries. In effect Russia has aligned itself with the nationalist and nativist right in European and American politics and the success of its future foreign policy depends on the success of this political tendency. It has undoubtedly chalked up some significant successes in recent years, especially around the toxic issue of immigration.

Russia has also sought to use economic means to reward its friends and punish its adversaries. This goes back to the early 1990s and has seemed a natural way to exert influence over countries that were also once members of the Soviet Union because of the extent of their economic dependence on Russia. Against vulnerable states these means could be successful. One example of successful coercion followed the shooting down of a Russian aircraft by Turkey in late 2015. In response, Russia imposed a number of sanctions on trade and travel between the two countries. In the summer of 2016, it got an apology from President Erdogan of Turkey, and relations went back to normal. The Russian approach to economic coercion has been to rely on real hurt to force change. In the case of Ukraine in 2013, it overreached. At first Putin got his way but the manner in which he did so, which underlined Yanukovych's weakness, provoked

a backlash that led to the loss of the most sympathetic government he was ever likely to get in Kiev. In the same way, by constantly exploiting the dependence of European customers for gas
supplies, it encouraged them to diversify their sources of supply.
When the Russians needed income as energy prices fell in 2014, it
found that its market share had decreased. Turning financial and
trade relationships into geopolitical instruments is rarely cost-
free. Customers lose trust and market mechanisms fail.

Since 2014, the West's use of economic sanctions has come
under more scrutiny. As already noted, they were valued at first
as much for their demonstrative as coercive effect, as a way of
objecting to what Russia was doing in Ukraine. This demonstrative effect is why sanctions are adopted as a first step when military measures would be inappropriate and imprudent. Those
imposing sanctions, however, would rarely claim that the purpose is solely to make a point and not get the target to change
behavior. The normal accusation against Western sanctions is
that although they represented the main coercive pressure on
Moscow, they had very little effect in practice. Russia did not back
down on Ukraine. Western economic and political interests were
harmed, with lost investment opportunities, especially in the energy sector. Russia was encouraged to diversify and develop new
partnerships and financial instruments independent of the West.
Despite claims that they were targeted, ordinary people were still
hurt as the Russian government cut social spending. The West
was blamed for the hardships.[14] The sanctions had more impact
than intended because they coincided with a drop in the oil price.
In combination, this was a major shock to the Russian economy.
They were targeted against Putin's close associates, but he did not,
as a result, abandon these figures; instead he drew them closer

and excluded the more liberal voices on Russia's economy who sought to calm relations with the West. One conclusion therefore was that while sanctions undoubtedly did have significant impacts, policy makers could "overestimate their ability to calibrate and control these tools of economic statecraft."[15] Russia never suggested that it was indifferent to sanctions. It pressed to have them reversed and objected to plans for their extension. While they had no direct coercive effect in forcing Russia to back down, they may have had some deterrent effect and helped set limits to the Russian intervention, although this was unlikely to have been the main reason why Russia did not push much farther into Ukraine. The extent to which successful coercion depends on the target's economic vulnerability was best illustrated by the IMF's ability to keep pushing Ukraine to reform its economy and address corruption once it needed the Fund's support and had nowhere else to turn. In the IMF's case the starting point was not a threat but the inducement of substantial loans, but once the IMF could threaten to withhold further payments then the position was tantamount to coercion.

For all its innovative features, the lessons from the Russo-Ukrainian for strategic art are both old and generally negative:

- It is far easier to start a war than to end one. To end a war started thoughtlessly and going badly means losing face, which is why governments prefer to find some semistable equilibrium that avoids the impression of loss even though it offers no prospect of victory.
- Brute force still matters in a fight over territory.
- Superior firepower can gain territory but is of little help in its administration. "Hearts and minds" must

therefore be taken into consideration. If the population is hostile and uncooperative, then they can be encouraged to flee. Thus the Assad regime in Syria, backed by Russia, was prepared to retake contested areas by forcing civilians out, whereas in Ukraine, despite the large numbers of people displaced by the fighting, this was not the intention. The Russians wished to claim that the population welcomed their liberation from the "Kiev Junta." The need for receptive populations limited Russia's ability to advance beyond the enclaves of Donetsk and Luhansk.

- Winning support in contested areas requires credible local leadership. Russian efforts were handicapped from the start by the lack of such leadership. There was a tension from the outset between the desire of those leading the enclaves to get as close as possible to Russia and the Russian preference for them to play the role of spoilers within the Ukrainian political system.

- There are always ways to hurt and embarrass opponents, and their suffering may have value. But acts of revenge rarely translate into positive achievements while modest forms of pressure may serve as no more than statements of disapproval. Effective coercion requires a vulnerable target that will struggle to cope with the pressure but also clear demands so that the target knows what to do. It is possible to have too much coercive effect, for the very act of compliance, especially when conspicuous and contested, will weaken the target government. Euromaidan was the result of Moscow being prepared to destabilize its protégé Yanukovych in order to keep him in line.

- Disruptive cyberattacks and social media campaigns can leave opponents disoriented but not necessarily compliant. Over time they will adapt and become more resilient. Instruments of coercion are likely to lose their impact as the targets learn to adapt. Moreover, when the sources of the campaign wish to stay anonymous and attribution is denied then the target will be unsure whether any concessions may make a difference, and the pressure will lose its impact. Once a cyber attack is over, even if it causes real disruption, there may not be a natural next step. Most obviously, it is not a way to take territory or change a government.

- Should a stalemate develop and the conflict become calmer then the pressure to settle will be reduced. Once outside powers begin to assume that a conflict can be contained, the urgency will go out of their efforts at mediation and peace-making. These efforts require considerable commitments of time and energy, and even some forms of pressure if the belligerents are to be persuaded to offer concessions. France and Germany used their influence in the Minsk process to help set the framework for an eventual deal, but this only slowed down the pace of the fighting. Its main effect, with which they were probably content, was to confirm the conflict's boundaries so that it was less likely that the conflict would have wider repercussions.

- When a state is being pulled in two different directions then a definitive choice either way is bound to cause some turmoil. To prevent a conflict escalating the simplest remedy for external powers may be to discourage such a choice, to "freeze" a conflict at whatever stage it has reached when a ceasefire is reached. The effect may just be to perpetuate internal paralysis. Decisions become scrutinized for what they imply about future changes in political alignments without the deadlock ever being broken. The problem for 'buffer states' is that they are apt to get buffeted. Sometimes the only long-term solution is to accept that a country has chosen a new political alignment.

- The ability to cope with a protracted conflict, especially one that has become a contest of fatigue, lies in economic performance. The biggest failure of Ukrainian strategy was to use the Russian threat as a reason to let up on domestic reform and anticorruption.

- Sometimes clever strategy and innovative techniques can push out the limits, and more will be obtained than could reasonably have been expected. That is not what happened with Russia and Ukraine. The basic lesson is that with limited war you don't always get what you want. Nor do you get much satisfaction.

NOTES

INTRODUCTION

1. Lawrence Freedman, *Strategy: A History* (New York: Oxford University Press, 2013).
2. John Mearsheimer, "Why the Ukraine Crisis Is the West's Fault," *Foreign Affairs* 93, no. 5 (2014): 84.
3. Lawrence Freedman, "Ukraine and the Art of Crisis Management," *Survival* 56, no. 3 (May 2014): 7–42; "Ukraine and the Art of Limited War," *Survival* 56, no. 6 (November 2014): 7–38; "Ukraine and the Art of Exhaustion," *Survival* 57, no. 5 (October 2015): 75–106.
4. There is now a substantial literature covering the conflict from a variety of angles. This list is not exhaustive: Tim Judah, *In Wartime: Stories from Ukraine* (London: Allen Lane, 2015); Taras Kuzio, *Putin's War against Ukraine: Revolution, Nationalism, and Crime* (CreateSpace, 2017); Rajan Menon and Eugene Rumer, *Conflict in Ukraine: The Unwinding of the Post–Cold War Order* (Cambridge, MA: MIT Press, 2015); Constantine Pleshakov, *The Crimean Nexus and the Clash of Civilizations* (New Haven, CT: Yale University Press, 2017); Richard Sakwa, *Frontline: Crisis in the Borderlands* (London: I. B. Tauris, 2016); Gerard Toal, *Near Abroad: Putin, the West, and the Contest over Ukraine and the Caucasus* (New York: Oxford University Press, 2017); Shaun Walker, *The Long Hangover: Putin's New Russia and the Ghosts of the Past* (Oxford: Oxford University Press, 2018); Mikhail Zygar, *All the Kremlin's Men: Inside the Court of Vladimir Putin* (New York: PublicAffairs, 2016); Agnieszka Pikulicka-Wilczewska and Richard Sakwa, eds., *Ukraine and Russia: People, Politics, Propaganda, and Perspectives* (Bristol: E-International Relations Publishing, 2015), http://www.e-ir.info/

wp-content/uploads/2016/06/Ukraine-and-Russia-E-IR-2016.pdf.
Andrew Wilson, *The Ukraine Crisis: What It Means for the West* (New Haven: Yale University Press, 2014).

5. For the clash of competing narratives, see, for example, Sakwa, *Frontline*, and Kuzio, *Putin's War*.

CHAPTER 1

1. Ariel Alexovich, "Clinton's National Security Ad," *New York Times* (blog), February 29, 2008, http://thecaucus.blogs.nytimes.com/2008/02/29/clintons-national-security-ad/?_php=true&_type=blogs&_php=true&_type=blogs&_php=true&_type=blogs&_php=true&_type=blogs&_r=3.

2. See, for example, Phil Williams, *Crisis Management: Confrontation and Diplomacy in the Nuclear Age* (London: Martin Robertson, 1976); Michael Brecher and John Wilkenfeld, *A Study of Crisis* (Ann Arbor: University of Michigan Press, 2000).

3. The only source for this is Coral Bell's *Conventions of Crisis: A Study in Diplomatic Management* (Oxford: Oxford University Press, 1971); I have never found any other corroboration; McNamara also repudiated the concept: "'Managing' crises is the wrong term; you don't 'manage' them because you *can't* 'manage' them," James G. Blight and David A. Welch, *On the Brink: Americans and Soviets Reexamine the Missile Crisis* (New York: Farrar, Strauss and Giroux, 1989), 99.

4. Secretary of State John Foster Dulles, interview with James Shepley, *Life*, January 16, 1956.

5. The term may well have been inspired by Stephen Potter's humorous book *Gamesmanship* (1947); Hugh Rawson and Margaret Miner, eds., *The Oxford Dictionary of American Quotations* (Oxford: Oxford University Press, 2006), 269; in 1965, P. G. Wodehouse published *The Brinkmanship of Galahad Threepwood*; the term is still in use and in connection with the Ukraine crisis, for example, in an editorial in the London *Times*, April 11, 2014.

6. Michael Dobbs, *One Minute to Midnight: Kennedy, Khrushchev, and Castro on the Brink of Nuclear War* (New York: Alfred A Knopf, 2008).

7. Bruce W. MacDonald, *Looking Back on the Cuban Missile Crisis, 50 Years Later* (US Institute of Peace, October 19, 2012), http://www.usip.org/publications/looking-back-the-cuban-missile-crisis-50-years-later

8. I deal with this in Freedman, *Kennedy's Wars: Berlin, Cuba, Laos, and Vietnam* (New York: Oxford University Press, 2000).

9. The diplomat Harlan Cleveland observed in 1963: "You will have to live with the institutions you create. The law you make may be your own"; Harlan Cleveland, "Crisis Diplomacy," *Foreign Affairs* 41, no. 4 (July 1963): 638–49.

10. Lawrence Freedman, *Deterrence* (Cambridge, UK: Polity, 2005).

11. Alexander George and Richard Smoke, *Deterrence in American Foreign Policy: Theory and Practice* (New York: Columbia University Press, 1974), 11.

12. This distinction was first elaborated by Glenn Snyder in 1958, *Deterrence by Denial and Punishment* (Princeton, NJ: Center of International Studies, 1958); see Snyder, *Deterrence and Defense* (Princeton, NJ: Princeton University Press, 1961).

13. Robert Pape, "Coercion and Military Strategy: Why Denial Works and Punishment Doesn't," *Journal of Strategic Studies* 15, no. 4 (December 1992): 423–475.

14. For more on coercive diplomacy, see Alex George and William Simon, *The Limits of Coercive Diplomacy* (Boulder, CO: Westview Press, 1994); Lawrence Freedman, ed., *Strategic Coercion* (Oxford: Oxford University Press, 1998).

15. Thomas Schelling, *Arms and Influence* (New Haven, CT: Yale University Press, 1966), 1–3; here he distinguishes between brute force and coercion, but it works with control.

16. Schelling, *Arms and Influence*, 79–80.

17. Schelling, *Arms and Influence*, 82.

18. Alexander L. George and William E. Simons, ed., *The Limits of Coercive Diplomacy* (Boulder, CO: Westview, 1994), 2, 13–14, 17–18; confusingly, George described coercive diplomacy as "defensive," but even within his own terms this does not really work.

19. George and Simons, *Limits*, 281, 293.

20. George and Simons, *Limits*, 18–19.

21. Gary Hufbauer, Jeffrey Schott, Kimberley Elliott, and Barbara Ogg, *Economic Sanctions Reconsidered*, 3rd ed. (Washington, DC: Institute for International Economics, 2007).

22. Juan Zarate, *Treasury's War: The Unleashing of a New Era of Financial Warfare* (New York: PublicAffairs, 2003).

23. Michael Brozska, "From Dumb to Smart? Recent Reforms of UN Sanctions," *Global Governance* 9 (2003): 519–535; David Cortright and George A. Lopez, eds., *Smart Sanctions: Targeted Economic Statecraft* (New York: Rowman & Littlefield, 2002).

24. *National Security Strategy* (Washington DC: The White House, February 2015).

25. Dan Drezner, "Economic Sanctions in Theory and Practice: How Smart Are They?" in *Coercion: The Power to Hurt in International Politics*, ed. Kelly M. Greenhill and Peter Krause, (New York: Oxford University Press, 2018), 257.

26. Drezner in Greenhill and Krause, *Coercion: The Power to Hurt*, 252.

27. Richard Nephew, *The Art of Sanctions* (New York: Columbia University Press, 2018), 144.

28. Brendan Taylor, "Sanctions as Grand Strategy," *Adelphi* 411 (London: Routledge for the International Institute for Strategic Studies, 2010).

29. Address by Prime Minister Begin at the National Defense College, August 8, 1982. http://www.mfa.gov.il/mfa/foreignpolicy/mfadocuments/year book6. Begin described the wars in 1956, when Israeli troops entered the Sinai Peninsula, and in 1967, when Israel began hostilities with a successful preemptive attack, which destroyed the Egyptian Air Force and began a Six-Day War, as the other wars of choice.

30. Richard Haass, *War of Necessity, War of Choice: A Memoir of Two Iraq Wars* (New York: Simon & Schuster, 2009).

31. Robert Endicott Osgood, *Limited War: The Challenge to American Strategy* (Chicago: University of Chicago Press, 1957).

32. This term was first coined in the late 1940s by the Hungarian Communist leader Matyos Rakosi to explain the political process by which the Soviet Union gained control of Eastern Europe. The Communists first organized "antifascist" governments that would then shut down the parties to the Right of them one by one, "cutting them off like slices of salami," until only the "end-piece" of the Communist Party remained. It was therefore about the progressive exclusion of opponents. Later in the Cold War the term tended to be used to refer to progressive but incremental victories. There is, however, one continuity here with the current Ukrainian crisis in the liberal use of the "fascist" label to delegitimize all other parties.

33. This is an old Chinese term that was employed by Mao Zedong, as when describing American imperialism: "In appearance it is very powerful, but in reality it is nothing to be afraid of; it is a paper tiger. Outwardly a tiger, it is made of paper, unable to withstand the wind and the rain. I believe that it is nothing but a paper tiger," Mao Zedong, "U.S.

Imperialism Is a Paper Tiger," July 14, 1956, https://www.marxists.org/
reference/archive/mao/selected-works/volume-5/mswv5_52.htm

34. This idea was not new. Consider Clausewitz: "war is an act of force,
     and there is no logical limit to the application of that force. Each side,
     therefore, compels its opponent to follow suit; a reciprocal action is
     started which must lead, in theory to extremes." Carl von Clausewitz,
     On War, ed. and trans. Michael Howard and Peter Paret (Princeton,
     NJ: Princeton University Press, 1976), 15.

35. Herman Kahn, *On Escalation: Metaphors and Scenarios* (New York:
     Praeger, 1965).

36. David Halberstam, *The Making of a Quagmire: America and Vietnam
     during the Kennedy Era* (New York: Random House, 1965).

37. Leslie Gelb and Richard Betts, *The Irony of Vietnam: The System Worked*
     (Washington, DC: Brookings Institution Press, 2001).

38. Gordon A. Craig, "Delbruck: The Military Historian," in *Makers of
     Modern Strategy: From Machiavelli to the Nuclear Age*, ed. Peter Paret
     (Princeton, NJ: Princeton University Press, 1986), 341–342. I deal with
     the legacy of Delbruck in Freedman, *Strategy: A History*.

39. David French, "The Meaning of Attrition, 1914–1916," *English Historical
     Review* 103, no. 407 (April 1988): 385–405.

40. Scott Sigmund Gartner and Marissa Edson Myers, "Body Counts and
     'Success' in the Vietnam and Korean Wars," *Journal of Interdisciplinary
     History* 25, no. 3 (Winter 1995): 377–395.

41. Yaacov Bar-Simon Tov, *The Israeli-Egyptian War of Attrition, 1969–70*
     (New York: Columbia University Press, 1980).

42. Carter Malkasian, *A History of Modern Wars of Attrition* (Westport,
     CT: Praeger, 2002); Malkasian's case studies involved campaigns
     within wider wars—for example, Britain's Burma campaign against the
     Japanese from 1942 to 1944 and the later stages of the Korean War.

43. J. Boone Bartholomees Jr., "The Issue of Attrition," *Parameters*
     (Spring 2010), http://strategicstudiesinstitute.army.mil/pubs/parameters/
     Articles/2010spring/40-1-2010_bartholomees.pdf

CHAPTER 2

1.   This is not to argue that all the issues of Kosovo were settled at that
     point. Almost two decades later, however, Kosovo may be independent
     but it is hardly untroubled. Nor has Serbian nationalism died away.

2. "NATO Expansion: What Gorbachev Heard," *National Security Archive*, December 12, 2017, https://nsarchive.gwu.edu/briefing-book/russia-programs/2017-12-12/nato-expansion-what-gorbachev-heard-western-leaders-early.

3. William Safire, "Ukraine Marches Out," *New York Times*, November 18, 1991. The speech can be found at https://en.wikisource.org/wiki/Chicken__speech

4. NATO, *Partnership for Peace Programme*, https://www.nato.int/cps/en/natolive/topics_50349.htm

5. Mark Kramer, "The Myth of a No-NATO-Enlargement Pledge to Russia," *Washington Quarterly* 32, no. 2 (April 2009): 39–61.

6. Lincoln Mitchell, *The Color Revolutions* (Philadelphia: University of Pennsylvania Press, 2012).

7. Karen Dawisha, *Putin's Kleptocracy: Who Owns Russia?* (New York: Simon & Schuster, 2014).

8. Jeanne Wilson, "Colour Revolutions: The View from Moscow and Beijing," *Journal of Communist Studies and Transition Politics* 25, nos. 2 and 3 (June 2009): 369–395.

9. Eduard Shevardnadze, the president of Georgia who was overthrown in the Rose Revolution, had also spoken positively about the possibility of Georgia joining NATO; see Toal, *Near Abroad*, 100.

10. Another conflict was the result of a demand from the predominantly Armenian region of Nagorno-Karabakh, which demanded to be transferred from Azerbaijan to Armenia when both were part of the Soviet Union. Full-scale fighting erupted in 1992 as Nagorno-Karabakh took the opportunity to secede from Azerbaijan. Russia brokered a settlement in 1994, but there has been sporadic fighting ever since.

11. Address by Secretary General Manfred Wörner, "The Atlantic Alliance and European Security in the 1990s," https://www.nato.int/docu/speech/1990/s900517a_e.htm; this was in the context of the agreement on German unification, which included a pledge that: "Once Soviet forces had withdrawn, German forces assigned to NATO could be deployed in the former GDR, but foreign forces and nuclear weapons systems would not be deployed there." See Stephen Pifer, "Did NATO Promise Not to Enlarge: Gorbachev Says No," Brookings (blog), November 6, 2014, https://www.brookings.edu/blog/up-front/2014/11/06/did-nato-promise-not-to-enlarge-gorbachev-says-no/

12. Vladimir Putin, speech and the following discussion at the Munich Conference on Security Policy, February 10, 2007, http://archive.kremlin.ru/eng/speeches/2007/02/10/0138_type82912type82914type82917type84779_118123.shtml.

13. "Estonia and Russia: A Cyber-Riot," *Economist*, May 10, 2007; Matthew Crandall, "Soft Security Threats and Small States: The Case of Estonia," *Defence Studies* 14, no. 1 (March 2014): 30–55.

14. "I strongly believe that Ukraine and Georgia should be given MAP [Membership Action Plans], and there are no tradeoffs—period." Moscow immediately responded that this would upset the region's "strategic stability"; Luke Harding, "Bush Backs Ukraine and Georgia for NATO Membership," *Guardian*, April 1, 2008.

15. Condoleezza Rice, *No Higher Honor: A Memoir of My Years in Washington* (New York: Crown, 2011).

16. Vladimir Putin, "Questions Following a Meeting of the Russia-NATO Council," April 4, 2008, http://en.kremlin.ru/events/president/transcripts/24903.

17. Russia was, however, not successful in getting others to share its recognition of these secessionist entities; Russia was joined only by Nicaragua, Venezuela, Nauru, and Tuvalu.

18. The episode is fully discussed in Toal, *Near Abroad*.

19. Dmitry Medvedev, "Why I Had to Recognize Georgia's Breakaway Regions," *Financial Times*, August 26, 2008, https://www.ft.com/content/9c7ad792-7395-11dd-8a66-0000779fd18c.

20. "Remarks by the President at the New Economic School Graduation, Moscow, Russia," July 7, 2009, http://www.whitehouse.gov/the-press-office/remarks-president-new-economic-school-graduation

21. Kathryn Stoner and Michael McFaul, "Who Lost Russia (This Time)? Vladimir Putin," *Washington Quarterly* 38, no. 2 (2015): 167–187.

22. Embassy of the United States in Seoul, South Korea, "Remarks by President Obama and President Medvedev of Russia after Bilateral Meeting," transcript, March 27, 2012, cited in *Washington Quarterly* 38, no. 2: 176.

23. Tom Parfitt, "Anti-Putin Protestors March through Moscow," *Guardian*, February 4, 2012.

24. Michael Schwirtz and David Herszenhorn, "Russians Look at Election Results and Corruption Is What They See," *New York Times*, December 5, 2011.

25. Stoner and McFaul, "Who Lost Russia (This Time)?," 178.

26. https://www.pbs.org/wgbh/frontline/film/putins-revenge/transcript/

27. Amy Knight, "The Magnitsky Affair," *New York Review of Books*, February 22, 2018.

28. For an account of Ukraine's history, see Serhii Plokhy, *The Gates of Europe: A History of Ukraine* (London: Allen Lane, 2016).

29. Pleshakov, *Crimean Nexus*, 91.

30. Toal, *Near Abroad*, 199.

31. Anne Applebaum, *Red Famine: Stalin's War on Ukraine* (London: Allen Lane, 2017).

32. The poison was TCDD dioxin.

33. On Yanukovych's favorable policies towards Moscow see Andrei Tsygankov, "Vladimir Putin's Last Stand: the sources of Russia's Ukraine Policy", *Post-Soviet Affairs* 3, no. 4 (2015): 279–303. Anders Fogh Rasmussen, NATO's secretary-general, announced in October 2013 that Ukraine would not join the alliance in 2014.

34. Samuel Charap and Timothy J. Cotton, *Everyone Loses: The Ukrainian Crisis and the Ruinous Contest for Post Soviet Eurasia* (London: ISSS, 2006), 115.

35. Simon Tilford, "Poland and Ukraine: A Tale of Two Economies," *CER Bulletin* 95 (April/May 2014): 2–3.

36. Council of the European Union, *Joint Declaration of the Eastern Partnership Summit*, Warsaw, September 29–30, 2011.

37. Quoted in Charap and Colton, *Everyone Loses*, 100.

38. Putin insisted that this would not be incompatible with close ties with the EU and was not about "bringing back the Soviet Union"; Prime Minister Vladimir Putin, "A New Integration Project for Eurasia: The Future in the Making," *Izvestia*, October 3, 2011, http://www .russianmission.eu/en/news/article-prime-minister-vladimir-putin-new-integration-project-eurasia-future-making-izvestia-3-

39. This was reported as describing the collapse as "the" major geopolitical disaster, which gave a far starker meaning; Vladimir Putin, "Address to the Federal Assembly," April 24, 2005, http://archive.kremlin.ru/eng/speeches/2005/04/25/2031_type70029type82912_87086.shtml

40. Amanda Paul, "Russia Cranks Up Pressure on Ukraine," *Euobserver*, September 2, 2013; the European Parliament passed a resolution complaining of Russian pressure; see European Parliament resolution of September 12, 2013. On the Pressure Exerted by Russia on Eastern Partnership Countries (in the Context of the Upcoming Eastern Partnership Summit in Vilnius) (2013/2826(RSP)).

41. "Russia Threatens Moldova over Its EU Relations," *EurActiv.com*, September 3, 2013, http://www.euractiv.com/europes-east/russia-keeps-threatening-neighbo-news-530198; David M. Herszenhorn, "Russia Putting a Strong Arm on Neighbors," *New York Times*, October 22, 2013.

42. Charap and Colton, *Everyone Loses*, 116.

43. Mikael Wigell and Antto Vihma, "Geopolitics versus Geoeconomics: The Case of Russia's Geostratgy and Its Effects on the EU," *International Affairs* 92, no. 3 (2016): 2.

44. Daniel Drezner, *The Sanctions Paradox: Economic Statecraft and International Relations* (Cambridge: Cambridge University Press, 1999), 131–248. See Charap and Colton, *Everyone Loses*, 59.

45. Charap and Colton, *Everyone Loses*, 81.

46. The quote is from Vladimir Surkov, a close advisor of Putin; Pavel Baev, *Russian Energy Policy and Military Power: Putin's Quest for Greatness* (London: Routledge, 2008), 32.

47. Policy Department for External Relations, *Energy as a Tool of Foreign Policy of Authoritarian States, in Particular Russia* (European Parliament, April 2018), 14.

48. Wigell and Vihma, "Geopolitics Versus Geoeconomics, 2.

49. Jakob Hedenskog and Robert L. Larsson, *Russian Leverage on the CIS and the Baltic States* (Stockholm: FOI, 2007).

50. Gabriel Collins, *Russia's Use of the "Energy Weapon" in Europe*, Issue Brief (Houston, TX: Rice University, Baker Institute for Public Policy, July 18, 2017).

51. Karen Smith Stegen, "Deconstructing the 'Energy Weapon': Russia's Threat to Europe as a Case Study," *Energy Policy* 39, no. 10 (2011): 6505–6513.

52. Interestingly, these were the Zaporozhye, Dnepropetrovsk, and Odessa regions, rather than the parts of Donbas area that eventually came to be controlled by the separatists; see the interview of Sikorski by Ben Judah, "Putin's Coup: How the Russian Leader Used the Ukraine Crisis to Consolidate His Dictatorship," *Politico Magazine*, October 19, 2014, http://www.politico.com/magazine/story/2014/10/vladimir-putins-coup-112025.html#ixzz3Gh3SNyUQ.

53. Shaun Walker, "Vladimir Putin Offers Ukraine Financial Incentives to Stick with Russia," *Guardian*, December 18, 2013, https://www.theguardian.com/world/2013/dec/17/ukraine-russia-leaders-talks-kremlin-loan-deal

54. The IMF suggested that its terms had been overstated and that reforms could be introduced gradually, but it still insisted that more relief was conditional on more reform, http://en.interfax.com.ua/news/economic/183315.html

55. David Herszenhorn, "Ukraine Blames I.M.F. for Halt to Agreements with Europe," *New York Times*, November 22, 2013.

56. http://www.forbes.com/sites/kenrapoza/2014/04/03/russia-helped-ukraine-but-now-ukraine-needs-more-imfs-lagarde-says/

57. Gunta Pastore, "The EU-Ukraine Association Agreement Prior to the Vilnius Eastern Partnership," *Baltic Journal of European Studies* 4, no. 2 (2017): 16.

58. See http://cpi.transparency.org/cpi2013/

59. Ambrose Evans-Pritchard, "Historic Defeat for EU as Ukraine Returns to Kremlin Control," *Telegraph*, November 22, 2013. On why the EU missed the signs fo a developing crisis see forthcoming book by Christoph O. Meyer, Chiara de Franco, and Florian Otto, *Heeding Warnings about Violent Conflict? Persuasion in Foreign Policy*.

60. Arseniy Yatseniuk, "Ukraine to Sign Customs Union Accession Deal on Dec 17—Opposition Leader," *Interfax-Ukraine*, December 7, 2013, http://en.interfax.com.ua/news/general/179960.html; this was denied by a Kremlin spokesman even though issues of trade and finance were being discussed; "Putin, Yanukovych Didn't Discuss Ukraine Joining Customs Union—Kremlin Spokesman," *Voice of Russia*, December 7, 2013, https://sputniknews.com/voiceofrussia/news/2013_12_07/Putin-Yanukovych-didnt-discuss-Ukraine-joining-to-Customs-Union-Kremlin-spokesman-8639/

61. Walker, "Vladimir Putin Offers Ukraine Financial Incentives."

62. Serhiy Leshchenko, "Yanukovych's Secret Diaries," *Euromaidan Press*, March 12, 2014.

63. On the potential as seen at the time for escalating violence see https://www.bbc.co.uk/news/world-europe-26265808.

64. "Agreement on Settlement of the Crisis in Ukraine," Kiev, February 21, 2014, http://www.auswaertiges-amt.de/cae/servlet/contentblob/671350/publicationFile/190051/140221-UKR_Erklaerung.pdf.

65. Stephen Pifer and Hannah Thoburn, "Victor Yanukovych: Losing Europe…and Losing the Ukrainian Public," Brookings (blog), November 18, 2013, https://www.brookings.edu/blog/up-front/2013/11/18/viktor-yanukovych-losing-europe-and-losing-the-ukrainian-public/

66. See, for example, "Poll: More Ukrainians Disapprove of Euromaidan Protests Than Approve of It," *Kiev Post*, February 7, 2014, https://www.Kievpost.com/article/content/ukraine-politics/more-ukrainians-disapprove-of-euromaidan-protests-than-approve-of-it-poll-336461.html

67. Considerable controversy still surrounds the responsibility for the mass killings on February 20. The official Ukrainian view is that most deaths were the responsibility of a special unit of the Berkut riot police acting on the orders of Yanukovych, but there are alternative claims, promoted on Russian media outlets, that it was the responsibility of individuals connected with Euromaidan as a "false flag" operation. On how social media was used to demonstrate the responsibility of Berkut officers for these deaths see Mattathias Schwartz, "Who Killed the Kiev Protestors? A 3-D Model Holds the Clues," *The New York Times Magazine*, May 30, 2018.

68. A pro-Bandera march on January 1, 2014, attracted fifteen thousand supporters, while the main march had two hundred thousand.

69. The transcript can be found at http://www.bbc.co.uk/news/world-europe-26079957

70. Walker, "Vladimir Putin Offers Ukraine Financial Incentives," 129.

71. Yanukovych's corruption is fully described on a site that draws on documents that were recovered from the lake at Mezhiyhirya; see http://yanukovychleaks.org/en/

72. For a clear presentation of Moscow's view, which stops short of actual endorsement, see Dmitri Trenin, "The Crisis in Crimea Could Lead the World into a Second Cold War," *Observer*, March 2, 2014.

CHAPTER 3

1. Foreign Minister Sergey Lavrov's remarks and answers to media questions at the Primakov Readings International Forum, Moscow, June 30, 2017, http://www.mid.ru/en/meropriyatiya_s_uchastiem_ministra/-/asset_publisher/xK1BhB2bUjd3/content/id/2804842

2. See Toal, *Near Abroad*, 208.

3. Daniel Treisman, "Why Putin Took Crimea: The Gambler in the Kremlin," *Foreign Affairs*, 95, no. 3 (May/June 2016): 47–55.

4. During the Cold War this was described as "Finlandization," referring to the postwar deal with the Soviet Union whereby Finland was able to adopt a democratic system and a market economy in return for making sure it remained friendly to the Soviet Union in its foreign policy. It became a term of abuse, initially in Germany, employed against those who seemed to be ready to give Moscow a veto over foreign policy in return for a quiet life. The term was revived in connection with Ukraine's predicament; Richard Milne, "'Finlandization' Makes a Polarizing Comeback in Finland," *Financial Times*, September 24, 2014.

5. Shaun Walker reported at the time that Putin's decisions pointed to "reactive, adhoc and impulsive moves rather than the implementation of a strategic gambit long in the planning". "Ukraine and Crimea: what is Putin thinking?" *The Guardian*, 23 March 2014.

6. Timothy Snyder, *The Road to Unfreedom* (London: Bodley Head, 2018), 135–37. In February 2015, a Ukrainian paper published a report supposedly circulated in Moscow prior to Yanukovych's flight combining a damning portrayal of the then president with claims that the protests were orchestrated by Polish and British intelligence. It suggested that the country was close to disintegration, and that much of Eastern Ukraine as well as Crimea was ready to integrate with Russia. "Novaya

Gazeta's 'Kremlin Papers' article: Full text in English," UNIAN, February 25, 2015, https://www.unian.info/politics/1048525-novaya-gazetas-kremlin-papers-article-full-text-in-english.html

7. The Russian foreign minister Sergey Lavrov discussed these proposals on Russia's state television program *Sunday Times* (*Vremya Voskresnoe*) on March 30, 2014. The response of the Ukrainian ministry of foreign affairs was posted on their website on March 30, http://euromaidanpr.com/2014/03/30/ukraines-foreign-ministry-responds-to-russias-demands-for-federalization/

8. Cited by Zygar, *All the Kremlin's Men*.

9. A poll conducted by a Crimean firm on March 8–11 showed 97.7 percent support for annexation; Toal, *Near Abroad*, 222.

10. http://www.bbc.co.uk/news/world-europe-26613567;http://www.whitehouse.gov/the-press-office/2014/03/17/fact-sheet-ukraine-related-sanctions

11. Vladimir Putin answered journalists' questions on the situation in Ukraine, March 4, 2014, http://eng.kremlin.ru/news/6763

12. Treisman, "Why Putin Took Crimea," 52–53.

13. Walker, *Long Hangover*.

14. Address by the president of the Russian Federation, March 18, 2014, http://eng.kremlin.ru/news/6889

15. Paul Sonne, "Five Things Putin Had to Say about Ukraine," *Wall Street Journal* (blog), April 17, 2014, http://blogs.wsj.com/five-things/2014/04/17/5-things-putin-had-to-say-about-ukraine/

16. Quoted in Carl Bildt, *Is Peace in Donbas Possible?* (European Council on Foreign Relations, October 12, 2017).

17. International Republican Institute, *Public Opinion Survey Residents of Ukraine March 14–26, 2014*, http://www.iri.org/sites/default/files/2014%20April%205%20IRI%20Public%20Opinion%20Survey%20of%20Ukraine,%20March%2014-26,%202014.pdf

18. See http://www.bbc.co.uk/news/world-europe-26400035

19. See https://www.cbsnews.com/news/aid-to-russia-leader-vladimir-putin-claims-us-giving-ukraine-rebels-20-million-a-week/

20. Dmitri Simes, "An Interview with Sergey Glazyev," *National Interest*, March 24, 2014. On Galyev as an exponent of "schizofascism" (denouncing others as fascist while following fascistic policies) see Snyder, *The Road to Unfreedom*, 146–47

21. See http://uaposition.com/analysis-opinion/english-translation-audio-evidence-putins-adviser-glazyev-russian-politicians-involvement-war-ukraine/

22. Andrew Roth, "From Russia, 'Tourists' Stir the Protests," *New York Times*, March 3, 2014.

23. https://www.rferl.org/a/kharkiv-operation-ukraine-terrorism-separa-tist-arrests/25324984.html

24. Marck Rachkevych, "Armed Pro-Russian Extremists Launch Coordinated Attacks in Donetsk Oblast, Seize Regional Police Headquarters, Set Up Checkpoint," *Kyiv Post*, April 12, 2014.

25. Interview with Zavtra in November 2014; Anna Dolgov, "Russia's Igor Strelkov: I Am Responsible for War in Eastern Ukraine," *Moscow Times*, November 21, 2014.

26. "Stalemate: Ukraine and Russia Are Both Trapped by the War in Donbas," *Economist*, May 27, 2017.

27. Toal, *Near Abroad*, 264.

28. "Who Are You, the Shooter?" Conversation between chief editor of *Tomorrow*, Mr. Prokhanov, and Mr. Igor Strelkov, former defense minister of Donetsk People's Republic, November 20, 2014, https://igorstrelkov.wordpress.com/2014/11/20/who-are-you-the-shooter-interview-with-igor-strelkov/

29. Kirit Radia, "NATO Commander Offers Evidence of Russian Troops in Ukraine," ABC (blog), April 17, 2014, http://abc-news.go.com/blogs/headlines/2014/04/nato-commander-offers-evidence-of-russian-troops-in-ukraine/.

30. Paul Sonne, "Five Things Putin Had to Say about Ukraine," *Wall Street Journal* (blog), April 17, 2014, http://blogs.wsj.com/five-things/2014/04/17/5-things-putin-had-to-say-about-ukraine/

31. US ambassador Power at United Nations: "[T]he government of Ukraine has acted with restraint in the face of repeated provocations." Remarks by Ambassador Samantha Power, US Permanent Representative to the United Nations, at a Security Council stakeout on Ukraine, March 15, 2014, http://usun.state.gov/briefing/statements/223543.htm

32. Mat Babiak, "A Report on Kiev International Institute for Sociology, Data from April 8–16, 2014," *Ukraine Policy*, April 20, 2014, http://ukrainianpolicy.com/southeast-statistics-of-ukraine-april-2014/

33. Neil Macfarquhar, "Under Russia, Life in Crimea Grows Chaotic," *New York Times*, April 21, 2014, http://www.nytimes.com/2014/04/22/world/europe/under-russia-life-in-crimea-grows-chaotic.html?hpw&rref=world&_r=0. Of particular concern was a water shortage, which threatened Crimea's harvest: http://www.bbc.co.uk/news/world-europe-27155885

34. See http://www.themoscowtimes.com/news/article/russia-sees-need-to-protect-russian-speakers-in-nato-baltic-states/507188.html

35. Justin Huggler, "Putin Privately Threatened to Invade Poland, Romania, and the Baltic States," *Daily Telegraph*, September 19, 2014.

36. Amy Knight, "Obama's Putin Delusion," *New York Review of Books* (blog), March 29, 2014, http://www.nybooks.com/blogs/nyrblog/2014/mar/29/obamas-putin-delusion/

37. See, for example, Marc Thiessen, "Obama's Weakness Emboldens Putin," *Washington Post*, March 3, 2014.

38. Nicholas Watt, "Ukraine: UK to Push for Tougher Sanctions against Russia over Crimea, *Guardian*, March 18, 2014.

39. Sam Jones, "Masterly Russian Operations in Ukraine Leave NATO One Step Behind," *Financial Times*, June 8, 2004.

40. Stephen Cohen, "Distorting Russia," *Nation*, March 3, 2014.

41. "A majority of 61 percent of Americans do not think the U.S. has a responsibility to do something about the situation between Russia and Ukraine, nearly twice as many as the 32 percent who think it does. . . . More specifically, 65 percent of Americans do not think the U.S. should provide military aid and equipment to Ukraine in response to Russia's actions, while only 26 percent think the U.S. should." CBS News, March 25, 2014, http://www.cbsnews.com/news/poll-most-say-us-doesnt-have-a-responsibility-in-ukraine/

42. http://www.themoscowtimes.com/news/article/russia-could-turn-us-into-radioactive-ashes-state-tv-anchor-says/496253.html

43. See http://www.telegraph.co.uk/news/worldnews/europe/russia/11064978/Ukraine-crisis-Putins-nuclear-threats-are-a-struggle-for-pride-and-status.html.

44. On the background to the nuclear deal, and why it made sense, see Tom Nichols, "Nuclear Weapons and the Ukraine Crisis," March 19, 2014, http://tomnichols.net/blog/2014/03/19/nuclear-weapons-and-the-ukraine-crisis/

45. Maria Rost Rublee, "Fantasy Counterfactual: A Nuclear-Armed Ukraine," *Survival* 57, no. 2 (2015): 145–56.

46. Steven Pifer notes that both assurances and guarantees translate as guarantees in Ukrainian and Russian; Pifer, *The Eagle and the Trident: U.S.-Ukraine Relations in Turbulent Times* (Washington, DC: Brookings Institution Press, 2017).

47. The treaty also referred to "the protection of the ethnic, cultural, linguistic, and religious originality of national minorities on their territory" and the creation of "conditions for the encouragement of that originality."

48. Philip Pan, "Ukraine's Extension of Russia Base's Lease May Challenge U.S. Goals in Region," *Washington Post*, April 28, 2010.

49. https://www.un.org/apps/news//story.asp?NewsID=47362&Cr=Ukrain e&Cr1=, https://www.un.org/News/Press/docs/2014/ga11493.doc.htm

50. http://thecable.foreignpolicy.com/posts/2014/04/10/un_hints_russia_ and_its_allies_rigged_crimeas_secession_vote

51. http://www.bbc.co.uk/news/world-europe-26613567; http://www. whitehouse.gov/the-press-office/2014/03/17/fact-sheet-ukraine-related-sanctions

52. These included prohibitions on new debt or new equity greater than thirty days' maturity to identified persons operating in the Russian financial sector; new debt greater than ninety days' maturity to identified persons operating in the Russian energy sector; the export of goods, services (except for financial services), or technology in support of exploration or production for deep-water, Arctic offshore, or shale products that have the potential to produce oil in Russia, to identified persons operating in the Russia energy sector; and on new debt greater than thirty days' maturity to identified persons operating in the Russian defense sector.

53. Remarks by President Obama and German Chancellor Merkel in Joint Press Conference, May 2, 2014, https://obamawhitehouse.archives.gov/ the-press-office/2014/05/02/remarks-president-obama-and-german-chancellor-merkel-joint-press-conference

54. Secretary of State John Kerry, press conference after meeting Russian foreign minister Lavrov, March 14, 2014, http://www.state.gov/ secretary/remarks/2014/03/223523.htm

55. Council of the European Union. "Council Conclusions on Ukraine," *Foreign Affairs Council Meeting*, Brussels, March 17, 2014.

56. "NATO Flexes Its Muscle in Response to Crimea Crisis," *EurActiv*, April 2, 2014, http://www.euractiv.com/sections/global-europe/nato-flexes-its-muscle-response-crimea-crisis-301302

57. http://www.rferl.org/content/russia-nato-baltics-nordics-/26952328. html; Paul Belkin, Derek E. Mix, Steven Woehrel, "NATO: Response to the Crisis in Ukraine and Security Concerns in Central and Eastern Europe," *Congressional Research Service*, April 16, 2014, http://www.fas. org/sgp/crs/row/R43478.pdf

58. Michael D. Shear, "Obama Rules Out Military Force over Ukraine," *New York Times*, March 20, 2014.

59. Andrew Higgins and Neil MacFarquhar, "Ukraine President Says Europe's Security Depends on Stopping Russia," *New York Times*, August 30, 2014.

60. Kiran Stacey, George Parker, and Christian Oliver, "Business Frustrates Sanctions Push," *Financial Times*, April 17, 2014.

61. "The West must understand that, to Russia, Ukraine can never be just a foreign country." Henry Kissinger, "How the Ukraine Crisis Ends," *Washington Post*, March 5, 2014.

62. Charap and Colton, *Everyone Loses*, 131.

63. "Joint Geneva Statement on Ukraine from April 17: The Full Text," *Washington Post*, April 18, 2014.

64. See the website of the OSCE mission on http://www.osce.org/ ukraine-smm/

65. The political section of the planned Association Agreement was signed on March 21, 2014. The remaining sections, notably the Deep and Comprehensive Free Trade Area, was scheduled to be signed after Ukraine's presidential elections, http://eeas.europa.eu/ukraine/index_ en.htm

66. "International Monetary Fund staff endorsed a $17 billion loan to Ukraine to help the government pay its debts amid a projected economic contraction of 5 percent this year." See http://www.bloomberg .com/news/2014-04-23/imf-staff-said-to-back-17-billion-ukraine-loan-amid-contraction.html

67. President Obama in Estonia on September 3: "Since ultimately there's no military solution to this crisis, we will continue to support President Poroshenko's efforts to achieve peace because, like all independent nations, Ukraine must be free to decide its own destiny"; remarks by President Obama to the People of Estonia, Tallinn, Estonia, White House: Office of Press Secretary, September 3, 2014, http://www.whitehouse.gov/the-press-office/2014/09/03/remarks-president-obama-people-estonia.

68. "Western Delusions Triggered This Conflict and Russians Will Not Yield," *Financial Times*, September 14, 2014.

69. The referendums were held on May 11, 2014. They took place even after Putin had asked that they be postponed. It was claimed that 2,252,867 had voted in favor of self-rule, with 256,040 against, on a turnout of nearly 75 percent. The 89 percent "yes" vote was in line with what had apparently been suggested in an intercepted call with the organizers and a Russian politician, but out of line with recent opinion polling in the region. See http://en.wikipedia.org/wiki/Donbas_ status_referendums,_2014

70. "Putin the Uniter," *Economist*, June 20, 2015, http://www.economist .com/news/europe/21654663-war-has-made-most-ukrainians-see-russians-enemies-not-friends-putin-uniter

71. Survey by the Kiev International Institute of Sociology. It did not include areas under Russian/separatist control. http://khpg.index .pphp?id=1437504890org/. The figure willing to give up Crimea was higher at 33 percent, but still much lower than the 50.6 percent against.

72. On the role of volunteer battalions in the Ukrainian military effort see Ilmari Käihkö, "A Nation-in-the-Making: Control of Force, Strategy, and the Ukrainian Volunteer Battalions," *Defence Studies* 18, no. 2 (2018): 147–66. Part of the appeal of the volunteer battalions was that they were not part of the state, which remained distrusted by much of Ukrainian civil society. The Right Sector was prominent in organizing volunteers for the front line, which supported the more critical narratives of the Ukrainian campaign. Over time the government worked to integrate these groups into the army, despite the suspicions between the two.

73. "Ukraine President Poroshenko Hails 'Turning Point,'" BBC, July 6, 2014, http://www.bbc.co.uk/news/world-europe-28180907

74. Strelkov interview, as quoted in *Moscow Times* (see n 24, this chapter).

75. Glasykov's alarm at the developing situation can be seen in a June 2014 analysis, https://wikispooks.com/wiki/Document:US_is_militarizing_ Ukraine_to_invade_Russia

76. Ankit Panda, "Malaysian Airlines Flight MH17 Shot Down over Donetsk, Ukraine," *Diplomat*, July 18, 2014, http://thediplomat.com/ 2014/07/malaysian-airlines-flight-mh17-shot-down-over-donetsk-ukraine/. For a full analysis of what Russian sources said about this incident, see Aric Toler, "The Kremlin's Shifting, Self-Contradicting Narratives on MH17," *Bellingcat*, January 5, 2018, https://www .bellingcat.com/news/uk-and-europe/2018/01/05/kremlins-shifting-self-contradicting-narratives-mh17/.

77. http://www.telegraph.co.uk/news/worldnews/europe/russia/11732678/ One-year-on-MH17-evidence-against-separatists-appears-over-whelming.html; "MH17 Crash: Russia Vetoes UN Resolution for Criminal Tribunal," http://www.bbc.co.uk/news/world-europe-33710088

78. http://www.nytimes.com/2014/08/20/world/europe/plenty-of-room-at-the-top-of-ukraines-fading-rebellion.html

79. Sergei Loiko, "The Unraveling of Moscow's 'Novorossia Dream,'" RFE/ RL, June 1, 2016.

80. Walker, *Long Hangover*, 218.

81. One allegation was that a purpose was to extract from Ukraine such material from defense plants necessary for Russian defense production; Reuben Johnson, "Russian Aid Convoy Committed Wide-Scale Looting, Says Ukraine," *IHS Jane's Defence Weekly*, August 27, 2014.

82. http://www.huffingtonpost.com/2014/08/28/ukraine-russia_n_
     5728738.html, *Financial Times*, August 16, 2014, http://www.telegraph
     .co.uk/news/worldnews/europe/germany/angela-merkel/11060559/
     Serving-Russian-soldiers-on-leave-fighting-Ukrainian-troops-along-
     side-rebels-pro-Russian-separatist-leader-says.html
83. http://www.cfr.org/ukraine/conversation-arseniy-yatsenyuk/
     p33512?cid
84. http://www.Kievpost.com/opinion/op-ed/osce-releases-the-12-
     point-protocol-agreements-reached-between-ukraine-russia-and-
     separatists-in-minsk-363816.html
85. "Ukraine's Election: Springboard for Change?," IISS: *Strategic
     Comments*, October 13, 2014; a poll carried out in September 2014 by
     the International Foundation for Electoral Systems (IFES) showed that
     Ukrainians remained evenly divided on whether a military (40%) or a
     negotiated solution (41%) was preferable.
86. Terrence McCoy, "What Does Russia Tell the Mothers of Soldiers Killed
     in Ukraine? Not Much," *Washington Post*, August 29, 2014.
87. http://www.ibtimes.com/russia-risks-recession-after-economic-
     sanctions-over-ukraine-crisis-1695692; http://www.forbes.com/sites/
     paulroderickgregory/2014/08/28/western-sanctions-and-rising-
     debts-are-already-strangling-the-russian-economy/
88. For the dependency of individual countries, see *New York Times* chart,
     updated, September 2, 2014, http://www.nytimes.com/interactive/
     2014/03/21/world/europe/how-much-europe-depends-on-russian-en-
     ergy.html?_r=1
89. http://rt.com/politics/official-word/196284-ukraine-putin-
     nazi-europe/
90. "Russian Sanctions Could Be Eased Soon If Ukraine Progress
     Made: U.S. Adviser," Reuters, October 10, 2014; the link with Crimea
     was less clear.
91. "Crimea Seeks Billions from Moscow to Aid Investment Projects,"
     Moscow Times, September 15, 2014.
92. http://www.bbc.co.uk/news/world-europe-29290246
93. http://www.bbc.co.uk/news/world-europe-29342463
94. "Fight Club," *Economist*, October 11, 2014.
95. http://www.telegraph.co.uk/news/worldnews/europe/ukraine/
     11169790/Ukraine-peace-plan-blow-as-rebels-reject-Donetsk-and-
     Luhansk-autonomy-deal.html
96. http://en.ria.ru/world/20141018/194260010/Donetsk-Peoples-
     Republic-Likely-to-Remain-Formally-Unrecognized.html

97. http://www.theguardian.com/world/2014/oct/17/vladimir-putin-elections-ukraine-eu-leaders-minsk-peace

98. http://europa.eu/rapid/press-release_STATEMENT-14-276_en.htm; "Win Some, Lose More," *Economist*, September 20, 2014.

99. Peter Spiegel, "Putin Demands Reopening of EU Trade Pact with Ukraine," *Financial Times*, September 25, 2014.

100. United Nations Office for the Coordination of Humanitarian Affairs, Ukraine: Situation Report No. 15 as of October 10, 2014, http://reliefweb.int/report/ukraine/ukraine-situation-report-no-15-10-october-2014; these numbers include 298 from flight MH17 (see URL below) and depend on reports from official sources and medical establishments and are likely to be underestimates; Office of the United Nations High Commissioner for Human Rights, *Report on the Human Rights Situation in Ukraine*, September 16, 2014, 3, http://www.ohchr.org/Documents/Countries/UA/OHCHR_sixth_report_on_Ukraine.pdf; the report attributed civilian deaths to indiscriminate shelling of residential areas by both pro-Russian separatists and by the Ukrainian armed forces.

101. According to one report the Russian troops are the most capable units on the anti-Ukrainian side, with the regular Donetsk and Luhansk rebel formations being used essentially as "cannon fodder," Igor Sutyagin, *Russian Forces in Ukraine*, (London: RUSI March 2015).

102. http://www.nytimes.com/2015/01/23/world/europe/ukraine-cedes-donetsk-airport-to-rebels-as-fighting-continues.html?_r=2 .

103. http://www.bbc.co.uk/news/world-europe-31519000;   Andrew E. Kramer and David M. Herszenhorn, "Retreating Soldiers Bring Echoes of War's Chaos to a Ukrainian Town," *New York Times*, February 20, 2015.

104. United Nations Security Council Resolution 2202 (2015), available at http://www.un.org/press/en/2015/sc11785.doc.htm; see also "Protocol on the Results of the Consultations of the Trilateral Contact Group regarding Joint Measures Aimed at the Implementation of the Peace Plan of the President of Ukraine P. Poroshenko and Initiatives of the President of the Russian Federation V. Putin," available at http://www.osce.org/home/123257; "Memorandum on the Implementation of the Protocol on the Results of the Consultations of the Trilateral Contact Group Regarding Joint Measures Aimed at the Implementation of the Peace Plan of the President of Ukraine P. Poroshenko and Initiatives of the President of the Russian Federation V. Putin," available at http://www.osce.org/home/123806

105. "Militia Leader Not Sure If Unrecognized Luhansk Republic Will Remain Part of 'New Ukraine,'" *TASS*, February 18, 2015, http://tass.com/world/778404

106. http://www.reuters.com/article/2015/04/30/us-usa-defense-europe-idUSKBN0NL2ED20150430

107. http://en.interfax.com.ua/news/general/264224.html; see Mark Urban, "How Many Russians Are Fighting in Ukraine," BBC, March 10, 2015, http://www.bbc.co.uk/news/world-europe-31794523

108. http://www.janes.com/article/51295/saceur-analysts-see-russia-renewing-invasion-of-ukraine-in-next-two-months.

109. http://www.unocha.org/top-stories/all-stories/five-things-you-need-know-about-crisis-ukraine

110. http://www.reuters.com/article/2015/06/03/us-ukraine-crisis-clashes-idUSKBN0OJ1DJ20150603

111. http://www.bbc.co.uk/news/world-europe-33003237

112. http://uk.reuters.com/article/2014/11/12/uk-ukraine-crisis-military-idUKKCN0IW17P20141112; http://www.reuters.com/article/2015/04/30/us-usa-defense-europe-idUSKBN0NL2ED20150430

113. This followed a meeting of the Normandy group of France, Germany, Ukraine, and Russia on July 24, http://www.interpretermag.com/ukraine-live-day-526-sbu-and-lawyers-deny-claims-that-captured-spetsnaz-soldiers-have-been-exchanged/#9300

114. http://www.unian.info/politics/1091188-poroshenko-says-russia-changes-tactics-towards-ukraine.html; Poroshenko, June 18, 2015: "Poroshenko says that if earlier the Russian Federation counted on military success along the contact line, it has now set a task to intensify subversive activity inside Ukraine amid the increased efficiency and combat capacity of the Ukrainian army."

115. Pavel K. Baev, "How Long Can Putin Continue Doing Nothing?" *Eurasia Daily Monitor* 12, no. 140 (July 27, 2015), http://www.jamestown.org/single/?tx_ttnews%5Btt_news%5D=44217&tx_ttnews%5BbackPid%5D=7&cHash=26baf8e3c01771b0a7f956b3076c97c7#.VbeSP_lVhHw

116. A publication at the end of June 2015 listed the names and other information relating to 435 Russians killed in Ukraine, http://www.evasiljeva.ru/2015/06/30062015.html

117. http://www.bbc.co.uk/news/world-europe-32913929

118. http://news.yahoo.com/dozens-russian-troops-flee-unit-fearing-ukraine-deployment-182036031.html

119. http://www.defensenews.com/story/defense/international/europe/2015/07/25/-war-ukraine-military--modernize-past-soviet-era/30625241/

CHAPTER 4

1. President Obama: "The future of Syria must be determined by its people, but President Bashar al-Assad is standing in their way." White House (blog), August 18, 2011, https://obamawhitehouse.archives.gov/blog/2011/08/18/president-obama-future-syria-must-be-determined-its-people-president-bashar-al-assad

2. Michael Kofman and Matthew Rojansky, "What Kind of Victory for Russia in Syria?" *Military Review Online Exclusive* (January 2018), http://www.armyupress.army.mil/Portals/7/Army-Press-Online-Journal/documents/Rojansky-Russia-Victory-a.pdf. See also Dmitri Trenin, *What Is Russia up to in the Middle East* (Cambridge: Polity, 2018).

3. Putin's U.N. General Assembly speech, *Washington Post*, September 28, 2015, https://www.washingtonpost.com/news/worldviews/wp/2015/09/28/read-putins-u-n-general-assembly-speech/?utm_term=.8be67e530884

4. "Egypt's President Admits Russian Plane Downed by 'Terrorism,'" *Gulf Today*, February 24, 2016, http://gulftoday.ae/portal/33ce7bab-4b9c-499e-89c2-bac4ae1454af.aspx

5. "Turkey's Downing of Russian Warplane—What We Know," BBC, December 1, 2015, http://www.bbc.co.uk/news/world-middle-east-34912581

6. "Russia Places Sanctions on Turkey," *New York Times*, November 29, 2015.

7. "Erdogan 'Sorry' for Downing of Russian Jet," *Al Jazeera*, June 27, 2016, http://www.aljazeera.com/news/2016/06/turkey-erdogan-russian-jet-160627131324044.html

8. Colin P. Clarke and William Courtney, *View: Russia Trapped in Syria* (Santa Monica, CA: Rand Corporation, December 20, 2017), https://www.thecipherbrief.com/article/exclusive/middle-east/view-russia-trapped-syria

9. Reuters, "Syrian Delegates Refuse to Leave Airport on Arrival for Congress in Sochi Not Attended by US or UK," *Guardian*, January 30, 2018, https://www.theguardian.com/world/2018/jan/30/russia-syria-peace-conference-sochi-foreign-minister

10. Fred Kaplan, "The New Graveyard of Empires? Vladimir Putin's Grand Ambitions for Syria Aren't Working Out Quite as Planned," *Slate*, February 15, 2018, https://slate.com/news-and-politics/2018/02/vladimir-putins-grand-ambitions-for-syria-arent-working-out-quite-as-planned.html

11. https://www.opendemocracy.net/od-russia/mark-galeotti/chvk-wagner-and-privatisation-of-russian-geopolitics

12. Ellen Nakashima, Karen DeYoung, and Liz Sly, "Putin Ally Said to Be in Touch with Kremlin, Assad before His Mercenaries Attacked U.S. Troops," *Washington Post*, February 22, 2018. Thomas Gibbons-Neff, "How a 4-Hour battle between Russian Mercenaries and U.S. Commandos Unfolded in Syria," *New York Times*, May 24, 2018.

13. David E. Sanger and Steven Erlanger, "Suspicion Falls on Russia as 'Snake' Cyberattacks Target Ukraine's Government," *New York Times*, March 9, 2014.

14. Kim Zetter, "Inside the Cunning, Unprecedented Hack of Ukraine's Power Grid," *Wired*, March 3, 2016, https://www.wired.com/2016/03/inside-cunning-unprecedented-hack-ukraines-power-grid/. Another explanation was that it was a warning to the Ukrainian government not to nationalize privately owned power companies, some of which were owned by an oligarch close to Putin.

15. "Russian Military 'Almost Certainly' Responsible for Destructive 2017 Cyber Attack," *National Cyber Security Centre*, February, 15, 2018, https://www.ncsc.gov.uk/news/russian-military-almost-certainly-responsible-destructive-2017-cyber-attack

16. The group responsible was reported to be APT28, linked to Russia's GRU military intelligence agency and believed to be responsible for the attacks on Hillary Clinton's 2016 presidential campaign; "Cyberattack against German Government 'Ongoing,'" *AFP News*, March 1, 2018, https://sg.news.yahoo.com/cyberattack-against-german-Government-Ongoing-140846675.html. For the attacks on energy producers see Reuters, "German Intelligence Sees Russia behind Hack of Energy Firms: Media Report," June 20, 2018, https://uk.reuters.com/article/germany-cyber-russia/german-intelligence-sees-russia-behind-hack-of-energy-firms-media-report-idUKL8N1TM4XW

17. Alex Hern, "Ransomware Attack 'Not Designed to Make Money,' Researchers Claim," *Guardian*, June 28, 2017.

18. John P. Carlin, "Russia Is a Rogue State. Time to Say So," *Politico*, February 27, 2018, https://www.politico.com/magazine/story/2018/02/27/russia-election-meddling-rogue-state-217094

19. Nicole Kobie, "Nobody Is Safe from Russia's Colossal Hacking Operation," *Wired*, April 21, 2018, http://www.wired.co.uk/article/russia-hacking-russian-hackers-routers-ncsc-uk-us-2018-syria

20. "In the Kremlin's Pocket: Who Backs Putin and Why?" *Economist*, February 14, 2015.

21. Stefan Meister, "The 'Lisa Case': Germany as a Target of Russian Disinformation," *NATO Review*, July 2016.

22. http://www.theguardian.com/world/2015/jul/07/russia-propaganda-europe-america?CMP=share_btn_tw

23. "Russian Spies Hacked the Olympics and Tried to Make It Look Like North Korea Did It, U.S. Officials Say," Ellen Nakashima, *Washington Post*, February 24, 2018.

24. https://www.justice.gov/file/1035477/download; Andrei Sodatov, "How Vladimir Putin Mastered the Cyber Disinformation War," *Financial Times*, February 17, 2018; Anton Troinovski, "A Former Russian Troll Speaks: 'It Was Like Being in Orwell's World,'" *Washington Post*, February 17, 2018, https://www.washingtonpost.com/news/worldviews/wp/2018/02/17/a-former-russian-troll-speaks-it-was-like-being-in-orwells-world/?utm_term=.86141cfbe943; Alexander Reid Ross, "The Internet Research Agency," *Splcenter*, February 2018, https://www.splcenter.org/hatewatch/2018/02/21/internet-research-agency-behind-shadowy-network-meddled-2016-elections

25. https://panamapapers.icij.org/20160403-putin-russia-offshore-network.html

26. Vladimir Soldatkin, "Russia's Putin: Friend Named in Panama Papers Not Corrupt," *Reuters*, April 7, 2016, https://www.reuters.com/article/us-panama-tax-russia-putin/russias-putin-friend-named-in-panama-papers-not-corrupt-idUSKCN0X41L6

27. Julia Ioffe, "What Putin Really Wants," *Atlantic*, January/February 2018, https://www.theatlantic.com/magazine/archive/2018/01/putins-game/546548/

28. Robert D. Blackwill and Philip H. Gordon, *Containing Russia, Council Special Report*, no. 80 (New York: Council on Foreign Relations, January 2018). In an indictment filed in mid-July 2018 Mueller described how officers from Russian intelligence hacked the Democratic National Committee's server and passed its contents over to anti-Clinton organizations (including wikileaks).

29. Nick Confessore and Daisuke Wakabayashi, "Russians Spun American Rage into a Weapon," *New York Times*, October 10, 2017; Miriam Elder and Charlie Warzel, "Stop Blaming Russian Bots for Everything," *BuzzFeed*, February 28, 2018, https://www.buzzfeed.com/miriamelder/stop-blaming-russian-bots-for-everything?utm_term= .ym8MNmL3z#.foY0LYazX; for an argument that the Russian campaign did help turn the election, see Kathleen Hall Jamieson, *Cyberwar: How Russian Hackers and Trolls Helped Elect a President: What We Don't, Can't, and Do Know* (New York: Oxford University Press, 2018).

30. Intelligence Community assessment, *Background to "Assessing Russian Activities and Intentions in Recent US Elections": The Analytic Process and Cyber Incident Attribution*, January 6, 2017, https://www.dni.gov/files/documents/ICA_2017_01.pdf

31. Joint Statement from the Department of Homeland Security and Office of the Director of National Intelligence on Election Security, October 7, 2016, https://www.dhs.gov/news/2016/10/07/joint-statement-department-homeland-security-and-office-director-national

32. Franklin Foer, "The Plot against America: Paul Manafort and the Fall of Washington": "Decades before He Ran the Trump Campaign, Paul Manafort's Pursuit of Foreign Cash and Shady Deals Laid the Groundwork for the Corruption of Washington," *Atlantic*, March 2018, https://www.theatlantic.com/magazine/archive/2018/03/paul-manafort-american-hustler/550925/

33. Jeffrey Goldberg, "The Obama Doctrine," *Atlantic*, April 2006, https://www.theatlantic.com/magazine/archive/2016/04/the-obama-doctrine/471525/

34. Josh Rogin, "Trump Campaign Guts GOP's Anti-Russia Stance on Ukraine," *Washington Post*, July 18, 2016.

35. Josh Rogin, "Trump Administration Stalled on Whether to Arm Ukraine," *Washington Post*, October 29, 2017.

36. Aaron Mehta and Joe Gould, "Ukraine Officially Cleared to Buy Javelin Weapons," *Defense News*, March 1, 2018.

37. Jeremy Herb, "Senate Sends Russia Sanctions to Trump's Desk," July 28, 2017, http://edition.cnn.com/2017/07/27/politics/russian-sanctions-passes-senate/index.html

38. Nicole Gaouette, "Latest US Sanctions against Russia a Work in Progress," http://edition.cnn.com/2017/12/14/politics/trump-russia-sanctions-explainer/index.html

39. Neil MacFarquhar and Peter Baker, "Trump's Stance on Sanctions Angers both Moscow and Washington," *New York Times*, January 30, 2018.

40. Trump press conference, February 16, 2018: "I would love to be able to get along with Russia. Now, you've had a lot of presidents that haven't taken that tack. Look where we are now. Look where we are now. So, if I can—now, I love to negotiate things, I do it really well, and all that stuff. But—but it's possible I won't be able to get along with Putin." "Read a Transcript of President Trump's Combative Press Conference," *Time*, February 16, 2018.

41. Dina Smeltz, Lily Wojtowicz, and Stepan Goncharov, "American and Russian Opinion at a Standoff on Crimea Sanctions," *Chicago Council*

on *Global Affairs*, January 24, 2018, https://www.thechicagocouncil.org/publication/american-and-russian-opinion-standoff-crimea-sanctions#_ftn1

42. Peter Baker, "Trump Declines to Add Sanctions against Russians, Contradicting Haley," *New York Times*, April 6, 2018.

43. Tom Keatinge, "This Time, Sanctions on Russia Are Having the Desired Effect," *Financial Times*, April 13, 2018.

44. Neil MacFarquhar, "The Fight with the West Is Isolating Russia. But That Isn't Stopping Putin." *New York Times*, April 17, 2018.

45. Brian O'Toole, "Treasury Throws Russian Aluminum Giant a Lifeline," *Atlantic Council* (blog), April 23, 2018, http://www.atlanticcouncil.org/blogs/new-atlanticist/treasury-throws-russian-aluminum-giant-a-lifeline

46. Paul Taylor, "Trump's Next Target: NATO," *Politico*, June 18, 2018.

47. I. William Zartman and Maureen Berman, *Practical Negotiator* (New Haven, CT: Yale University Press, 1982).

48. "Revolution Devolution," *Economist*, December 9, 2017; Andrew Wilson, "Survival of the Richest: How Oligarchs Block Reform in Ukraine," *European Council on Foreign Affairs*, April 14, 2006, http://www.ecfr.eu/publications/summary/survival_of_the_richest_how_oligarchs_block_reform_in_ukraine6091

49. Anders Åslund, "Russia's War on Ukraine's Economy," *Project Syndicate*, July 10, 2015, http://www.project-syndicate.org/commentary/russia-war-on-ukraine-economy-by-anders-aslund-2015-07#jOQX863SD8PeOLAY.99

50. Anders Åslund, "Ukraine Must Put Reform Agenda in Overdrive While There's Still Time," *Atlantic Council* (blog), July 13, 2015, http://www.atlanticcouncil.org/blogs/new-atlanticist/ukraine-must-put-reform-agenda-in-overdrive-while-there-s-still-time

51. http://www.internal-displacement.org/europe-the-caucasus-and-central-asia/ukraine/figures-analysis

52. See http://www.nrcu.gov.ua/en/148/602750/

53. http://www.bloomberg.com/news/articles/2015-07-16/ukraine-passes-legislation-needed-for-next-slice-of-imf-bailout

54. https://en.hromadske.ua/posts/breaking-down-ukraines-new-occupied-territories-law

55. "Stalemate: Ukraine and Russia Are Both Trapped by the War in Donbas," *Economist*, May 27, 2017.

56. Paul Quinn-Judge, "The Revolution That Wasn't," *New York Review of Books*, April 19, 2018.

57. Andrew Higgins, "Crooked Deals as Kiev Fuels War Machine," *New York Times*, February 20, 2018.

58. See https://www.transparency.org/news/feature/corruption_perceptions_index_2017

59. Roman Olearchyk and Neil Buckley, "Finance Woes Hobble Ukraine's Recovery," *Financial Times*, February 6, 2018.

60. Christopher Miller, "Ukrainians Reflect Bitterly on 'Betrayed Hopes' of Euromaidan," RFE/RL (Radio Free Europe/Radio Liberty), December 29, 2017.

61. At the time NABU and the Specialized Anticorruption Prosecutor's Office were investigating 602 criminal proceedings and had sent 135 high-level cases to court. Daria Kaleniuk, "Actually the West's Anticorruption Policy Is Spot On," *Atlantic Council*, June 4, 2018. This was in response to Adrian Karatnycky and Alexander J. Motyl, "How Western Anticorruption Policy Is Failing Ukraine," *Foreign Affairs*, May 29, 2018, https://www.foreignaffairs.com/articles/ukraine/2018-05-29/how-western-anticorruption-policy-failing-ukraine

62. Center for Insights into Survey Research, Public Opinion Survey of Residents of Ukraine, November 15–December 14, 2017, http://www.iri.org/sites/default/files/2018-1-30_ukraine_poll_presentation.pdf

63. Ezekiel Pfeifer, "Russia's Currency Reserves: More Than Enough or Alarmingly Low?" *Institute of Modern Russia*, July 27, 2015, http://imrussia.org/en/analysis/economy/2362-russias-currency-reserves-more-than-enough-or-alarmingly-low

64. Pavel Felgenhauer, "'Party of War' Triumphs in Moscow," *Eurasia Daily Monitor* 14, no. 137 (October 26, 2017); see also *Eurasia Daily Monitor*, October 23, 2017.

65. Andrew E. Kramer, "Russia Is Returning to Growth (Just in Time for an Election)," *New York Times*, November 24, 2017.

66. See http://www.consilium.europa.eu/en/press/press-releases/2015/06/19-crimea-eu-extends-restrictions-illegal-annexation/

67. See https://www.whitehouse.gov/the-press-office/2015/06/08/g-7-leaders-declaration

68. Dina Smeltz, Lily Wojtowicz, and Stepan Goncharov, "American and Russian Opinion at a Standoff on Crimea Sanctions," *Chicago Council on Global Affairs*, January 24, 2018, https://www.thechicagocouncil.org/publication/american-and-russian-opinion-standoff-crimea-sanctions#_ftn1

69. Anders Åslund, "Russia Is in No Economic Shape to Fight a War," *Moscow Times*, April 22, 2014, http://www.themoscowtimes.com/

opinion/article/russia-is-in-no-economic-shape-to-fight-a-war/
498728.html.

70. http://bigstory.ap.org/article/f01ca72ac74d4956beb2b1046714121e/
us-eu-ready-tough-russia-sanctions-case-theyre-needed

71. http://www.washingtonpost.com/blogs/monkey-cage/wp/2015/01/28/
russia-is-hinting-at-a-new-cold-war-over-swift-so-whats-swift/

72. Sergey Karaganov, "Western Delusions Triggered This Conflict and
Russians Will Not Yield," *Financial Times*, September 14, 2014.

73. Leslie Gelb and Dimitri Simes had argued that such an alliance was
possible even before the Ukraine crisis in "Beware Collusion of China,
Russia: U.S. Policies Have Created a Risk of Pushing Two Great Powers
Together," *National Interest* (July–August 2013); for a more skeptical
view from early in the crisis, see "China and Russia: Best Frenemies,"
Economist, May 24, 2014.

74. Samuel Charap, John Drennan, and Pierre Noël, "Russia and
China: A New Model of Great-Power Relations", *Survival* 59, no. 1
(2017): 25–42. Peter Wood, "China-Russia Relations Reality Check,"
Jamestown Foundation, January 12, 2018, https://jamestown.org/pro-
gram/china-russia-relations-reality-check/

75. http://www.washingtonpost.com/blogs/monkey-cage/wp/2015/07/24/
hey-putin-have-you-seen-how-much-china-is-investing-in-ukraine/

76. https://www.dailysignal.com/2018/04/16/as-us-china-trade-war-
looms-ukraine-stands-to-gain/

77. In 2016, Prime Minister Dmitry Medvedev was caught in a video
responding to a Crimean pensioner complaining that her pension
was not keeping up with inflation. He responded: "There just isn't any
money now. When we find money, we'll make the adjustment." His
parting comment demonstrated his discomfort with the government's
failure to deliver on its early promises: "You hang in there. Best wishes!
Cheers! Take care!" "Medvedev's Awkward Crimea Moment: 'There's
Just No Money. But You Take Care!'" RFE/RL, May 24, 2016, https://
www.rferl.org/a/russia-medvedev-crimea-visit-no-money-social-
media-pensioner/27754644.html

78. Ridvan Bari Urcosta, "The Kerch Strait Bridge and Russia's A2/
AD Zone around Crimea," *Eurasia Daily Monitor* 15, no. 21
(February 12, 2018), https://jamestown.org/program/kerch-strait-
bridge-russias-a2-ad-zone-around-crimea/

79. The World Bank, Infographic: *Confidence Crisis Exposes Economic
Weakness in Russia*, March 26, 2014, http://www.worldbank.org/en/
news/feature/2014/03/26/infographic-rer31-confidence-crisis; http://

www.washingtonpost.com/world/europe/crimea-as-consolation-prize-russia-faces-some-big-costs-over-ukrainian-region/2014/03/15/a807ea20-230e-4f08-8d39-a8f090eb3fba_story.htm; http://www.reuters.com/article/2014/03/14/us-ukraine-crisis-idUSBREA1Q1E820140314; on gas markets, see Simon Pirani et al., "What the Ukrainian Crisis Means for Gas Markets" (paper presented at the Oxford Institute for Energy Studies, March 2014), http://www.oxfordenergy.org/wpcms/wp-content/uploads/2014/03/What-the-Ukraine-crisis-means-for-gas-markets-GPC-3.pdf

80. https://www.reuters.com/article/us-ukraine-gas-russia/ukraine-switches-power-plants-to-fuel-oil-closes-schools-to-save-gas-idUSKCN1GE1GC; Kenneth Rapoza, "In Shocking Turn of Events, Russia Now Owes Ukraine Billions," *Forbes*, March 1, 2018.

81. Gabriel Collins, "Russia's Use of the 'Energy Weapon' in Europe," Issue Brief (Houston, TX: Rice University, Baker Institute for Public Policy, July 18, 2017).

82. Rafal Bajczuk, "Germany: Closer to Approving the Construction of Nord Stream 2," *OSW* (Centre for Eastern Studies) (February 7, 2018), https://www.osw.waw.pl/en/publikacje/analyses/2018-02-07/germany-closer-to-approving-construction-nord-stream-2

83. Keith Johnson, "Is Germany Souring on Russia's Nord Stream?" *Foreign Policy*, April 10, 2018, https://foreignpolicy.com/2018/04/10/is-germany-souring-on-nord-stream-ukraine-gazprom/

84. See https://euobserver.com/foreign/141584, Ambrose Evans-Pritchard, "Gazprom Is an Arm of Kremlin Foreign Policy and Strategic Reach," *Daily Telegraph*, April 12, 2018; https://www.telegraph.co.uk/business/2018/04/12/leaked-eu-files-show-brussels-cover-up-collusion-putins-gazprom/

85. http://www.bloomberg.com/news/articles/2015-06-16/putin-s-economic-aides-fret-about-what-he-won-t-tell-investors

86. http://www.reuters.com/article/2015/06/19/us-russia-crisis-putin-economy-idUSKBN0OZ17U20150619?irpc=932

87. https://www.washingtonpost.com/blogs/worldviews/wp/2015/06/24/putins-approval-ratings-hit-89-percent-the-highest-theyve-ever-been/

88. http://imrussia.org/en/analysis/politics/2286-the-myth-of-putins-89

89. "Enter Tsar Vladimir," *Economist*, October 28, 2017; there were also suggestions that this support was not wholehearted and weaker among educated middle classes and urbanites, http://imrussia.org/en/analysis/politics/2286-the-myth-of-putins-89

90. For an excellent overview see Keir Giles, Philip Hanson, Roderic Lyne, James Nixey, James Sherr, and Andrew Wood, *The Russian Challenge*, Chatham House Report, June 2015, http://www.chathamhouse.org/sites/files/chathamhouse/field/field_document/20150605RussianChall engeGilesHansonLyneNixeySherrWoodUpdate.pdf

91. http://www.corriere.it/english/15_giugno_07/vladimir-putin-interview-to-the-italian-newspaper-corriere-sera-44c5a66c-0d12-11e5-8612-1eda5b996824.shtml

92. http://tass.ru/en/world/802259

93. http://www.themoscowtimes.com/opinion/article/rebel-infighting-bringing-chaos-to-east-ukraine/526305.html

94. Franklin Holcomb, *The Kremlin's Irregular Army: Ukrainian Separatist Order of Battle* (Washington, DC: Institute for the Study of War, September 2017), 10.

95. Holcomb, *Kremlin's Irregular Army*, 11.

96. Paul Quinn-Judge, "The Revolution That Wasn't," *New York Review of Books*, April 19, 2018.

97. "Ukraine Conflict: Poroshenko Calls for UN Peacekeepers," February 19, 2015, http://www.bbc.co.uk/news/world-europe-31527414

98. Alexander Vershbow, *How to Bring Peace to the Donbas (Yes, It's Possible)*, Atlantic Council, January 5, 2018.

99. Elizabeth Pond, "War in Ukraine: Is This the Way It Ends?," *Survival* 59, no. 6 (2017): 143; for detailed proposals, see Richard Gowan, *Can the United Nations Unite Ukraine?* (Washington, DC: Hudson Institute, February 2018).

100. Office of the United Nations High Commissioner for Human Rights (OHCHR), *Report on the Human Rights Situation in Ukraine, August 16 to November 15, 2017*, https://reliefweb.int/sites/reliefweb.int/files/resources/UAReport20th_EN.pdf

EVALUATION

1. Kimberley Marten, "Putin's Choices: Explaining Russian Foreign Policy and Intervention in Ukraine," *Washington Quarterly* 38, no. 2 (2015): 189; Michael Schwirtz, "Putin's Tips for What to Do When Negotiations Collapse," *New York Times*, October 7, 2016; Ukrainian president Poroshenko was also a judo enthusiast in his youth.

2. I explore this in Lawrence Freedman, *The Future of War: A History* (New York: PublicAffairs, 2017).

3. Luigi Scazzieri, "Europe, Russia and the Ukraine Crisis: The Dynamics of Coercion," *Journal of Strategic Studies*, 40, no. 3 (2017): 392–416.

4. Sam Jones, "Ukraine: Russia's New Art of War," *Financial Times*, August 28, 2014; Paul Goble, "Putin's Actions in Ukraine Following Script by Russian General Staff a Year Ago," *Interpreter*, June 20, 2014, http://www.interpretermag.com/putins-actions-in-ukraine-following-script-by-russian-general-staff-a-year-ago/; this was a speech from late January 2013 to the annual general meeting of the Russian Academy of Military Science on "The Role of the General Staff in the Organization of the Defense of the Country in Correspondence with the New Statute about the General Staff Confirmed by the President of the Russian Federation."

5. Paul Goble, "Russian Military Expert: Moscow Must Focus on Defending Itself against Hybrid Wars," *Eurasia Daily Monitor* 15, no. 40, March 15, 2018, https://jamestown.org/program/russian-military-expert-moscow-must-focus-defending-hybrid/.

6. Mark Galeotti, "I'm Sorry for Creating the 'Gerasimov Doctrine,'" *Foreign Policy*, March 5, 2018, https://foreignpolicy.com/2018/03/05/im-sorry-for-creating-the-gerasimov-doctrine/.

7. Samuel Charap, "The Ghost of Hybrid War," *Survival* 57, no. 6 (2015–16): 51–58. For history of the Russian concept see Ofer Fridman, *Russian "Hybrid War": Resurgence and Politicisation* (London: Hurst, 2018)

8. An example was the paramilitary Azov Battalion, which was linked to the Right Sector in Ukraine and was involved in the defense of Mariupol; Alec Luhn, "Preparing for War with Ukraine's Fascist Defenders of Freedom," *Foreign Policy*, August 30, 2014, http://www.foreignpolicy.com/articles/2014/08/30/Preparing_For_War_With_Ukraine_S_Fascist_Defenders_Of_Freedom; Valeriy Akimenko, *Ukraine's Toughest Fight: The Challenge of Military Reform* (Washington, DC: Carnegie Endowment for International Peace, February 2018).

9. Mark Rachkevych, "Ukrainian Air Force Has Lost 18 Combat Aircraft in Fighting with Rebels since April 2014," *Kyiv Post*, August 22, 2014.

10. Dmitry Adamsky, "From Moscow with Coercion: Russian Deterrence Theory and Strategic Culture," *Journal of Strategic Studies* 41, nos. 1–2 (2018): 33–60.

11. David Patrikarakos, *War in 140 Characters: How Social Media Is Reshaping Conflict in the Twenty-First Century* (New York: Basic Books, 2017).

12. See http://www.reuters.com/article/2015/01/21/us-ukraine-crisis-lavrov-idUSKBN0KU12Y20150121

13. Jolanta Darczewska, *The Devil Is in the Details: Information Warfare in the Light of Russia's Military Doctrine* (Warsaw: OSW, Centre for Eastern Studies, May 2015), http://www.osw.waw.pl/sites/default/files/

pw_50_ang_the-devil-is-in_net.pdf; Maksymilian Czuperski, John Herbst, Eliot Higgins, Alina Polyakova, and Damon Wilson, *Hiding in Plain Sight: Putin's War in Ukraine*, Atlantic Council, July 13, 2015, http://www.atlanticcouncil.org/publications/reports/hiding-in-plain-sight-putin-s-war-in-ukraine-and-boris-nemtsov-s-putin-war.

14. Emma Ashford, "Not-So-Smart Sanctions," *Foreign Affairs*, 95, no. 1, December 14, 2015, 114–23.

15. Peter Feaver and Eric Lorber, "The Sanctions Myth," *National Interest*, no. 138, June 15, 2015, 22–27.

INDEX

Abkhazia War (1992–93), 56
Adamsky, Dima, 177
Afghanistan, 59, 109, 116, 142
Akhmeoc, Rinant, 149
Aksyonov, Sergey, 90
Albania, 55
Aleppo (Syria), 131
Armenia, 68, 190n10
Assad, Bashar, 129, 131–32, 144, 182
attrition, 43–47. *See also* exhaustion
strategies
Austria, 71, 155
Azarov, Mykola, 74
Azerbaijan, 66, 190n10

Bakiev, Kurmanbek, 59
Baltic States. *See also* Estonia;
Latvia; Lithuania
European Union and, 106
North Atlantic Treaty
Organization and, 3, 54,
109, 146
North Stream gas pipelines and,
71, 156

Russian-speaking
community in, 99
Russia's energy trade with, 70
Soviet control (1940–91) of,
55, 104
Bandera, Stepan, 78, 92–93, 194n68
Barroso, José Manuel, 121
Bartholomees, Jr., J. Boone, 46
Begin, Menachem, 34, 188n29
Belarus, 66–68, 70–71, 99
Berlin Crisis (1961), 13, 15
Berlin Wall, 15, 53, 57
Black Sea fleet (Russia), 71, 86, 103
Blair, Tony, 52
Blinken, Tony, 117
Borodia, Alexander, 95
Bosnia-Herzegovina, 50, 53
Breedlove, Philip, 96, 124
Brest-Litovsk Treaty (1918), 61
Brexit campaign (United Kingdom,
2016), 179
brinkmanship, 14–15
Budapest Memorandum
(1994), 101–2